CRAZY-COOL
DUCT
TAPE
PROJECTS

Topiaries, page 120

CRAZY-COOL
DUCT
TAPE
PROJECTS

FUN AND FUNKY PROJECTS FOR FASHION AND FLAIR

Marisa Pawelko, Modern Surrealist

Design Originals

an Imprint of Fox Chapel Publishing

www.d-originals.com

ISBN 978-1-57421-424-6

Library of Congress Cataloging-in-Publication Data

Pawelko, Marisa.
  Crazy-cool duct tape projects / by Marisa Pawelko.
    p. cm.
  Includes index.
  ISBN 978-1-57421-424-6
  1. Tape craft. 2. Duct tape. I. Title.
  TT869.7.P39 2012
  745.59--dc23
                    2012021193

Printed in China
First Printing

About the Author

Meet celebrity crafter Marisa Pawelko, winner of the Craft & Hobby Association's Indie Craft and Crafty Couture Contests. Armed with a formal education in furniture design, Marisa used her talents to design products for the gift, toy, fashion, and accessories markets before turning her focus to the craft industry. In 2005, sparked with an idea to create a recycled baby memento-keeper out of one of her son, Joey's, baby food jars, she founded her company Modern Surrealist, which quickly developed an international following. Marisa enjoys inspiring crafters with thrifty project ideas and by "upcycling" ordinary objects into extraordinary custom creations. Marisa is an official crafter for the Duck® Brand duct tape. Her award-winning designs have been featured on PBS, HGTV, in the Illinois State Museum, and in countless exhibitions and high-end boutiques around the world. To learn more, please visit *www.modernsurrealist.com*.

Dedication

I dedicate this book to crafters around the world of all ages and walks of life!

I wish to thank everyone who has supported my endeavors over the years on this journey of creative exploration, and in particular, my very loving and supportive parents, Dulce and Bill, who have always believed in me and taught me to follow my heart while doing my very best work.

A special thank you to my inspiration and the light of my life, my wonderfully creative son and crafting partner, Joey: This is for you! Thank you for being such a wonderful person! May all your dreams come true as you continue to learn, grow, thrive, and craft!

To my best friend, sister, and brainstorming partner Christy: Thank you for all of your love, laughter, inspiration, and support! May you continue to reach for the stars!

To my darling Chris: Thank you for all of your loyal devotion, encouragement, patience, and love! I love and appreciate you with all of my heart!

To Westcott® Brand, VELCRO® Brand, The Duck® Brand, and Fox Chapel Publishing: Thank you for your continued support and for trusting in me to run with my many wild ideas!

—Marisa

CONTENTS

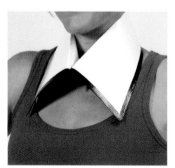

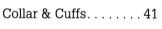

CHAPTER 2: TOO COOL FOR SCHOOL.........74

CHAPTER 3: DUCT TAPE DÉCOR 102

INTRODUCTION:
Ducking Around with Duct Tape

Duct tape is strong, durable, waterproof, and Army tested. In fact, duct tape was originally created during World War II as a product that allowed for rapid repair of Army supplies and vehicles. After the war's end, the civilian population embraced duct tape as a useful product for home repair and construction. Given the tape's versatility and durability, it's no surprise that people began experimenting with it to see what else it could do!

Out of this good-natured experimentation, the duct tape wallet was born. Duct tape became a popular medium for creating, and it made more than a few appearances on the tops of mortarboards at high school and college graduations. Duct tape dresses and tuxedoes began appearing more and more frequently at high school proms, spurred on by Duck® Brand's "Stuck at Prom" scholarship contest. The concept of covering items with duct tape, or making wearable items and accessories from it, became a rising trend that soon caught the attention of duct tape manufacturers.

To meet the needs of the growing and highly individualistic duct tape crafter population, Duck® Brand began producing tape in colors and patterns other than the familiar silver. Colored and patterned duct tape rolls were quickly followed by the invention of Duck® Brand's versatile and convenient duct tape sheets. These were readily embraced by crafters, who previously had to assemble their own duct tape sheets from individual strips of tape. Suddenly, duct tape was being stocked in the isles of craft superstores throughout the world.

Customers welcomed and were inspired by the new addition and its endless possibilities.

Duct tape crafting is quick, easy, affordable, mess-free, and requires no previous craft experience. Creative ideas and a willingness to experiment are all a novice crafter needs to get started. Crafting with duct tape is a fun-filled, creative, social activity that can be done in groups and is suitable for a range of ages. You can easily create all sorts of items that capture your individual style and also make great gifts for your friends and family! With duct tape crafting, there are no rules. You can make anything you want, in any color or pattern of tape you want, and if you make a mistake, just unstick your project, try again, and stick it back together; it's that easy.

The secret of mastering duct tape crafting is that you must learn to embrace the same type of creative experimentation that launched duct tape onto the craft scene—in other words, you have to learn to duck around! Ducking around with duct tape began a worldwide phenomenon that revolutionized the market for duct tape products. The new development inspired the creation of this book and is certainly part of the reason you are holding it in your hands. So let go of any lingering thought that duct tape crafts must be picture perfect and follow the instructions to the letter. Take hold of a brand new crafting philosophy and let your imagination run wild! After all, young or old, experienced crafter or craft novice, everyone enjoys the opportunity to duck around every now and again!

GETTING STARTED

Crafting with duct tape opens doors to limitless possibilities. You can use it for simple projects—like sprucing up an old photo frame by covering it in colored or patterned duct tape—or create more complex projects that primarily use duct tape and a handful of additional supplies. Such a range of possibilities might seem overwhelming. Where should you start?

This section introduces you to the basic tools, supplies, and techniques you'll need to create the projects in this book. Remember, crafting is mostly about experimenting. After much time spent refining my duct tape crafting techniques, I've found the materials, tools, and techniques listed here work best for me, but if you discover a different technique while working on a project—use it! The best thing about working with duct tape is there are no rules! So don't be afraid to experiment, make mistakes, or try something completely new.

Recommended Tools & Materials

I used the following tools and materials to create the projects in this book because of their unsurpassed quality, value, and effectiveness. Substitute your choice of brands, tools, and materials as desired.

ADTECH® BRAND HOT MELT GLUE PRODUCTS

❑ Mini High Temperature Glue Gun

❑ 5⁄16" x 4" (8 x 102mm) Mini Glue Sticks

BLUMENTHAL LANSING® BUTTONS

❑ Novelty Buttons

DARICE® BRAND EMBELLISHMENTS

❑ The Big Bling Gem Value Pack

DRITZ® BRAND NOTIONS FROM PRYM CONSUMER USA INC.

❑ Plastic Curtain Grommets

❑ Suspender/Mitten Clips

❑ Cover Button Kits

DUCK® BRAND DUCT TAPE

❑ Printed Duct Tape Rolls

❑ Color Duct Tape Rolls

❑ Printed Duct Tape Sheets

❑ Color Duct Tape Sheets

FLORACRAFT® BRAND FOAM PRODUCTS

❑ STYROFOAM™ Brand Foam

VELCRO® BRAND FASTENERS*

❑ VELCRO® Brand STICKY BACK™ Hook-and-Loop Fastener Strips

❑ VELCRO® Brand STICKY BACK™ Hook-and-Loop Fastener Coins

WESTCOTT® BRAND CUTTING TOOLS

❑ 8" (203mm) Titanium Bonded Non Stick Scissors

❑ 5" (127mm) Titanium Bonded Non Stick Scissors

❑ 3" (76mm) Titanium Bonded Scissors

❑ TrimAir Paper Trimmer

❑ Reversible Self-Healing Cutting Mat

❑ Cushion Grip Hobby Knife with Assorted Blade Shapes

❑ 12" (305mm) Stainless Steel Cork-Backed Ruler

❑ 18" (457mm) Stainless Steel Cork-Backed Ruler

*VELCRO® is a registered trademark of Velcro Industries B.V.

Basic Techniques

These nine techniques are the basic building blocks used to create every single project in this book. Once you master these simple skills, you'll be able to make and embellish anything you can imagine with duct tape, from wearable items to gifts to home décor and more!

PETAL POINTS

These little petal-like pieces of duct tape might seem simple and small on their own, but when assembled in colorful groups, they quickly transform into an eye-catching project. I used these handy pieces in various colors and patterns to make Petal Bracelets (page 32) and to cover the tops of Topiaries (page 124). You can use them any way you want, like to add a pointed fringe to a pair of Fingerless Gloves (page 59) or to add a scaled texture to the front of a Book Cover (page 92).

MEASURE AND CUT THE TAPE. Measure and trim a 3" (76mm)-long strip of duct tape from a roll.

MAKE THE FIRST FOLD. Flip the strip sticky side up and fold one of the front corners down along the long side of the tape. Make sure you are folding the tape so the sticky sides come together. Leave a small portion of the sticky side exposed along the edge of the strip.

MAKE THE SECOND FOLD. Fold the opposite front corner down so the tip of the strip forms a triangle. Press the edges down to secure the folded corners in place.

SOME SPECIAL TOOLS

CUTTING MAT

You will see that the tools list for almost every project in this book includes a cutting mat. While a cutting mat is not essential for each project, it is an incredibly useful. A cutting mat allows you to measure items without using a traditional ruler and to cut multiple items to a uniform length at the same time. It also makes a great work surface for assembling projects or for storing projects that are partially completed when you need to take a break.

NONSTICK SCISSORS

If you're working with duct tape, nonstick scissors are essential! They cleanly cut through sticky tape and never get gummed up or stuck to a project. When it comes to duct tape projects, nonstick scissors are a foolproof tool!

ADHESIVE ADVICE

See the Petal Bracelet project on page 32 for a great way to create multiple petal points quickly and efficiently .

FOLDED THIN STRIP

A folded thin strip takes the strength of duct tape and multiplies it by folding it over onto itself. Folded thin strips have finished edges and the ability to withstand wear and tear, so I use them for wearable pieces, such as the Suspenders on page 35, or projects that will see a lot of use, like the Purse on page 50. Never underestimate the power of folded thin strips to create cute (but durable!) projects.

Tools and Materials

- ❏ Duct Tape Roll
- ❏ Nonstick Scissors
- ❏ Cork-Backed Ruler
- ❏ Cutting Mat (optional)

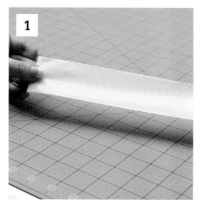

MEASURE AND CUT THE TAPE. Handling and folding very long strips of tape can be challenging for a beginning duct tape crafter. A good solution for this is to work with short strips of tape that can then be joined together (with more tape) to create long strips.

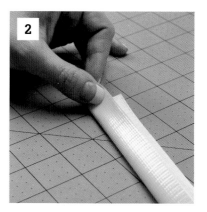

MAKE THE FIRST FOLD. Place the strip on your worktable, sticky side up. Fold it lengthwise, leaving a portion of the sticky side exposed along the edge of the strip.

ADHESIVE ADVICE

To avoid wrinkles and bubbles when making the first fold for a thin strip, start at the ends and work toward the middle, flattening the tape as you go. Any air bubbles in the tape will escape out the center.

MAKE THE SECOND FOLD. Starting in the middle and working toward the ends, fold the edge with the sticky side exposed down along the strip.

BOW

A bow is just one of the many embellishments you can incorporate into a variety of duct tape projects, and because it's made of duct tape, your bow will never rip, fray, or otherwise lose its beauty. Attach a magnet to the back of a bow to create a refrigerator decoration, or add some hook-and-loop fasteners to make an interchangeable piece that can easily be added and removed to adorn multiple items or projects.

Tools and Materials

- ❏ Duct Tape Roll
- ❏ Nonstick Scissors
- ❏ Cork-Backed Ruler
- ❏ Cutting Mat (optional)

MAKE A FOLDED THIN STRIP AND TRIM. Create a folded thin strip using the method described on page 14. Then, trim off a small section about 2" (51mm) long.

FORM A BOW. Shape the long folded thin strip into a bow.

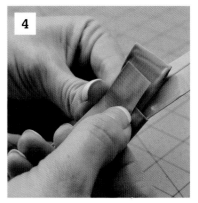

WRAP THE BOW. Wrap the small folded thin strip around the center of the bow.

SECURE THE BOW. Cut a small piece of duct tape from a roll and use it to secure the small folded thin strip in place.

ADHESIVE ADVICE

The length of the folded thin strip you use will determine the size of your finished bow. To make a large bow, use an extra-long folded thin strip.

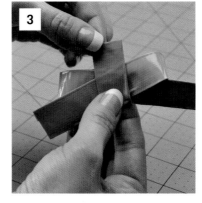

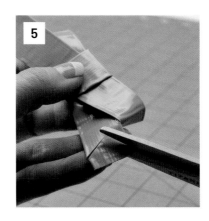

TRIM THE ENDS. Trim the ends of the bow as desired. You could leave them square, cut them at a 45-degree angle, or cut notches in them as shown.

WIDE STRIP

Like folded thin strips, wide strips are extra-strong. Wide strips are perfect for making oversize fringe. I used them for the Kilt (page 62) and the Halter Top (page 68). They also make great straps, or can be cut lengthwise to create a more traditional thin fringe. You can make wide strips the same color or pattern on both sides or match up different colors and patterns of tape for a unique reversible look.

Tools and Materials

- ❏ Duct Tape Roll
- ❏ Nonstick Scissors
- ❏ Cork-Backed Ruler
- ❏ Cutting Mat (optional)

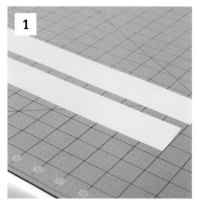

MEASURE AND CUT THE TAPE. From a roll of duct tape, measure and cut two strips of the same length. The length will vary by project.

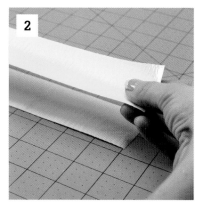

STICK THE STRIPS TOGETHER. Flip one strip over so the sticky side is up. Carefully align the second strip over the first, looking down on the strips from above to make sure your alignment is accurate. Make sure the sticky sides of the tape are facing each other. Lower the second strip onto the first and press them together.

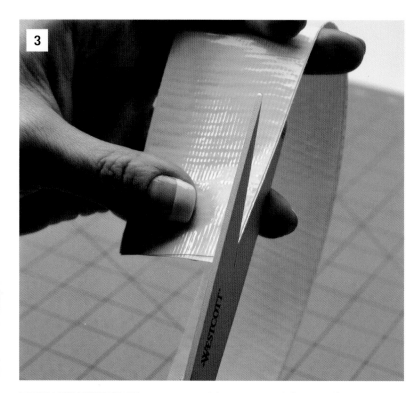

TRIM THE EXCESS. Trim away any sticky portions of the tape that are still exposed.

ADHESIVE ADVICE

Nonstick scissors are perfect for duct tape crafts, allowing you to trim away sticky portions of tape with ease.

RUFFLE

Ruffles make great embellishments for just about any project. I love to use ruffles as trim on wearable items like the Leg Warmers on page 55. Ruffles aren't just for clothing, though. I use them to add a decorative touch to my Topiaries (page 120) and other school and home décor items. You can easily patch ruffles together to make them as long as you want, so don't be afraid to add some pizzazz to a large project.

Tools and Materials

- ❏ Duct Tape Roll
- ❏ Duct Tape Sheet
- ❏ Nonstick Scissors
- ❏ Cork-Backed Ruler
- ❏ Cutting Mat (optional)
- ❏ Hot Glue Gun (optional)
- ❏ Glue Sticks (optional)

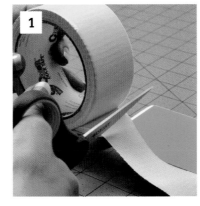

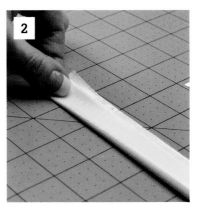

MEASURE AND CUT THE TAPE. Measure and cut a strip of duct tape from a roll. Ruffles are easily patched together to make long pieces, so I suggest starting out working with segments of tape no longer than 12" (305mm) at a time. Increase the length of the tape segments you use as you gain experience.

FOLD THE TAPE. Fold the strip lengthwise as you did for the folded thin strip (page 14), leaving a section of the back of the tape exposed along one of the edges. Fold the tape starting at the outer ends and working your way toward the center, using your thumbs.

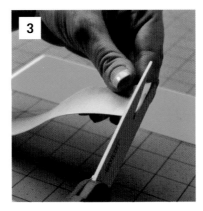

TRIM THE TAPE. Trim the ends of the strip to ensure they are straight. Also trim away any sticky backing that is exposed on the ends of the strip.

APPLY THE RUFFLE. Using the exposed sticky section on the back of your duct tape strip, apply the strip to your project, pressing the sticky edge of the strip against the project. Here, I'm attaching the strip to a duct tape sheet.

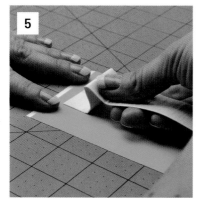

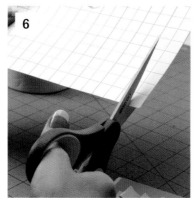

MAKE THE FIRST PLEAT. To create the pleats in the ruffle, fold the strip back on itself, pressing the sticky portion of the strip against the previous section of tape and against your project. You can vary the width of your pleats as desired. The ones shown are about ¾" (19mm) wide.

MEASURE AND CUT THE ANCHORING TAPE. Cut a strip from a sheet of duct tape the width of one row of squares printed on the back of the sheet. Cut the strip slightly longer than your ruffle. (You can also tear the strip lengthwise from a roll of duct tape.)

ADHESIVE ADVICE

To add more color to a ruffle, cut two anchoring pieces of tape and layer them along the edge of the ruffle.

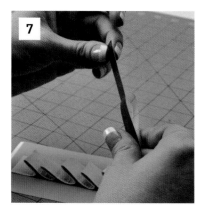

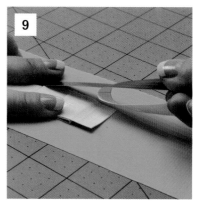

PEEL AWAY THE PAPER BACKING. Peel away a section of the paper backing from the anchoring strip. I find it easier to make my ruffles if I remove the paper backing a section at a time as I work.

BEGIN SECURING THE RUFFLE. Press the first few pleats of your ruffle flat, and place the strip along the top edge to secure them.

FINISH SECURING THE RUFFLE. Continue pressing the pleats of your ruffle down and securing them with the strip, removing the paper backing from the strip as you work. When you reach the end of the ruffle, trim off any extra length from the strip.

GLUE IF DESIRED. If the edge of the last pleat sticks up, you can use hot glue to secure it down flat.

SEAL THE EDGE. Run your fingernail along the edge of the ruffle to ensure a tight bond.

ADHESIVE ADVICE

If you have short nails, you can use the top of a pen or another object to seal the edge of the ruffle.

PATCHING A RUFFLE

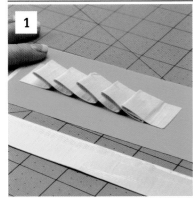

CUT A SECOND RUFFLE STRIP. If you want to extend your ruffle, measure and trim a second length of duct tape from a roll and fold it lengthwise as in Step 2 for making a ruffle.

APPLY THE SECOND STRIP. Lift up the edge of the last pleat of the ruffle you have already finished, and place the second strip underneath it, aligning it with the BOTTOM edge of your first ruffle.

PLEAT THE SECOND STRIP AND SECURE. Cover the patched section with the first pleat of the second strip. Continue pleating the strip until you reach the end. Add additional ruffle strips as desired until the ruffle reaches its finished length. Secure the edge of the ruffle with a strip from a duct tape sheet as described in steps 7–9 for making a ruffle.

DUCT TAPE STICKERS

Custom duct tape stickers are easy and fun to make, and you can cut them in any shape you desire. Make a simple sticker by cutting a shape from a sheet of duct tape. Apply your basic stickers to practically any surface. To create a sticker with multiple colors and dimensions, follow my instructions here. Layered stickers are a fast and easy way to bring a pop of color to any project.

Tools and Materials

- ❏ Duct Tape Sheets
- ❏ Nonstick Scissors
- ❏ Cork-Backed Ruler (optional)
- ❏ Cutting Mat (optional)

ADHESIVE ADVICE

The best way to remove the paper backing from a duct tape sheet is to place the sheet color side down and peel away the paper backing slowly so the sheet remains flat.

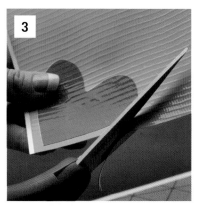

CUT THE FIRST SHAPE. Cut a shape from a sheet of duct tape. The shape I'm using is a heart.

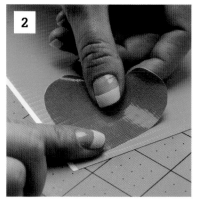

ATTACH THE SHAPE. Stick the first shape onto another sheet of duct tape with a different color or pattern.

CUT THE OUTLINE. Cut around the edges of your first shape, creating an even border.

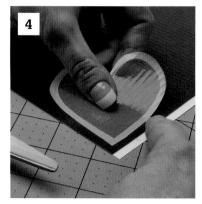

ATTACH THE SHAPE. Peel away the paper backing from the shape and attach it to a third sheet of duct tape with a different pattern or color.

CUT THE OUTLINE. Cut around the edges of the shape to create an even border. Use as many layers as you want, and experiment with different border widths. For a shadow effect, cut a thin border along one side of your shape and a thick border along the opposite side.

COVERED BUTTONS

Every crafter knows that buttons are not just for sewing! They make great additions to jewelry projects and accent details for picture frames, scrapbook pages, boxes, and more. What better way to celebrate the button's versatility than to cover it in duct tape to give it a bold new color and use it as part of a duct tape project? Duct-tape-covered buttons are perfect for rosette centers (see page 23) and make great finishing touches for wearable items. They're fabulously fashionable little embellishments that work just about anywhere. One of the best things about covered buttons is that you don't have to search for matching pairs or sets of buttons—you can make hundreds of identical buttons just by covering them in the same color or pattern of duct tape. If you want to mix and match, just use a different color or pattern. So easy, and so many possibilities! Note: For this project, you will need a cover button kit like those produced by Dritz®.

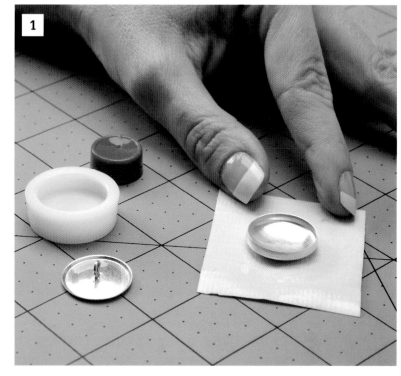

SELECT A BUTTON AND CUT THE TAPE TO SIZE. Select a button, and cut a strip of duct tape large enough to cover the button from a roll or sheet. Place the top of the button facedown in the center of the sticky side of the tape.

Tools and Materials

- ❑ Duct Tape Sheet or Roll
- ❑ Nonstick Scissors
- ❑ Cover Button Kit

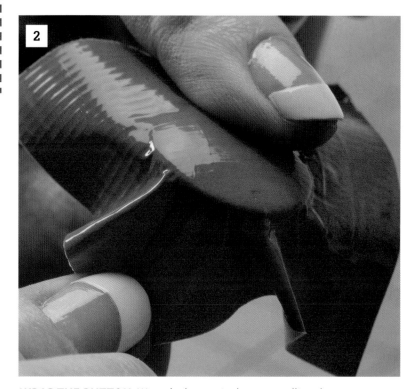

WRAP THE BUTTON. Wrap the button in the tape, pulling the tape taut over the button to eliminate any wrinkles.

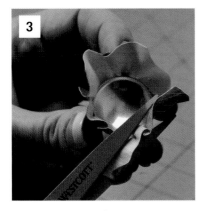

TRIM. Trim away the excess tape, leaving enough exposed to cover the sides and wrap around to the back of the button top.

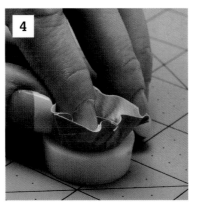

PLACE THE BUTTON TOP. Insert the button top facedown into the mold.

FOLD THE TAPE. Fold the edges of the tape down onto the back of button top.

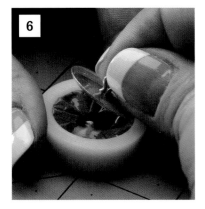

PLACE THE BUTTON BOTTOM. Put the bottom button piece in place on the back of the button top.

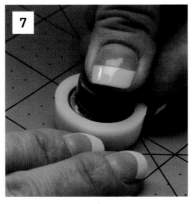

ASSEMBLE THE BUTTON. Use the pusher to push the button bottom into the button top, securing it.

REMOVE THE BUTTON. Use your fingers to gently push the finished button out of the mold. If desired, bend or trim the shank off the bottom of the button. You may also opt to use button bottoms that come without shanks.

BASIC ROSETTE

These flower-like creations will put you in embellishment heaven. You can stick them on *anything!* I like to use these as accent pieces on small projects, but you can also go crazy and use them to cover an entire surface like I did with the Water Bottle Chandelier (page 114). Add a magnet to the back and you can grow a rosette garden on your refrigerator or locker. And, as always with duct tape, the sky's the limit when it comes to color and pattern!

Tools and Materials

- ❏ Duct Tape Roll
- ❏ Nonstick Scissors
- ❏ Cork-Backed Ruler
- ❏ Hot Glue Gun
- ❏ Glue Sticks
- ❏ Accent Button or Gem
- ❏ Cutting Mat (optional)

ADHESIVE ADVICE

When working with hot glue, less is more. It is better to use too little and re-glue any pieces that may fall off than to use too much and risk creating a mess that is difficult to remove.

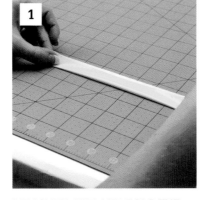

MEASURE, CUT, AND FOLD THE TAPE. Measure and trim an 8" (203mm)-long strip of tape from a roll. Fold the strip lengthwise as you did for the folded thin strip (page 14), leaving a portion of the sticky side exposed.

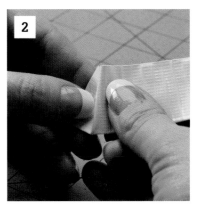

MAKE THE FIRST PLEAT. Flip the strip over and fold it at one end to create the first angled pleat. The sticky side of the tape will hold the pleat in place.

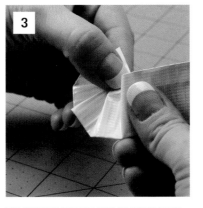

FINISH PLEATING THE ROSETTE. Continue making pleats, working the tape into a circle. It's helpful to keep your thumb in the center of the rosette as you form it to ensure the pleats stay in place.

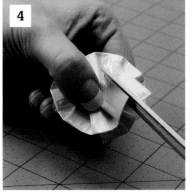

TRIM. When you complete the rounded pleating, trim away any excess from the end of the strip.

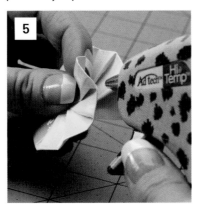

SECURE THE ROSETTE. Fold the end of the last pleat under to create a finished edge. If desired, use hot glue to secure the bottom of the last pleat in place.

ADD AN ACCENT PIECE. Glue a gem, covered button, or other accent piece into the center of the rosette.

LAYERED ROSETTE

While a basic rosette makes a cute accent piece you can use anywhere, a layered rosette is a bold piece that will really show off your duct tape skills. Layered rosettes are frilly, flirty, and super cute. These beautiful blooms will withstand much more wear and tear than a delicate fabric flower. Don't hesitate to add them to wearable items like headbands (see page 40) or frequently used items like handbags and shoes.

Tools and Materials

- ❏ Duct Tape Roll
- ❏ Duct Tape Sheet
- ❏ Nonstick Scissors
- ❏ Compass (optional)
- ❏ Cork-Backed Ruler
- ❏ Hot Glue Gun
- ❏ Glue Sticks
- ❏ Accent Button or Gem
- ❏ Cutting Mat (optional)

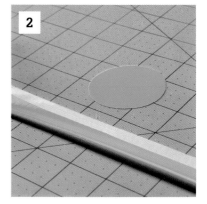

MEASURE AND CUT A CIRCLE. Cut a circle from a sheet of duct tape. Use a compass to draw the circle if you prefer not to draw freehand.

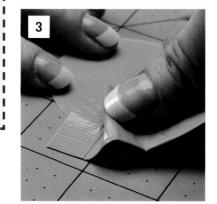

MEASURE AND CUT A STRIP. Measure and trim a 12" (305mm)-long strip from a roll of duct tape. Fold the strip lengthwise, leaving a portion of the sticky side exposed along the edge. Trim the ends to create clean edges.

BEGIN PLEATING. Apply the sticky edge of the strip to the circle you cut previously. Begin pleating the strip, working in a curve around the edge of the circle, adhering the sticky edge of the ruffle to the edge of the cut circle.

FINISH PLEATING. Continue pleating around the edges of the circle. If you run out of tape before you complete the circle, cut and fold a new strip of tape and patch it to the first ruffle, using the method described on page 19.

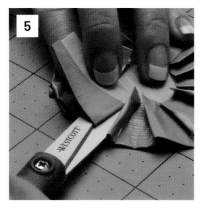

SECURE THE PLEATS. When you have finished pleating around the edges of the circle, trim any excess tape from the end of the last pleat. Tuck the end of the last pleat under the edge of the first pleat.

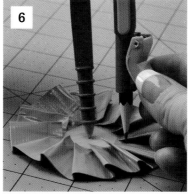

MEASURE AND CUT A SECOND CIRCLE. Cut another circle large enough to cover the center of the first circle and the edges of the pleats. If desired, hold a compass over the first rosette layer to determine the size of the circle you need.

PLACE THE SECOND CIRCLE. Remove the paper backing from the second circle, press the pleats flat, and secure the circle in place in the center of the first rosette layer. Make sure the edge of the circle overlaps the edges of the pleats.

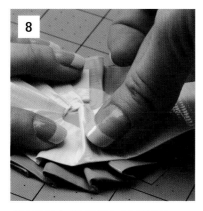

CREATE A SECOND ROW OF PLEATS. Measure and cut another 12" (305mm)-long strip of tape from a roll. Fold it lengthwise, leaving a portion of the sticky side exposed. Attach the sticky edge of the strip to the center circle of the rosette and pleat around the edge of the circle as you did with the first layer.

FINISH THE ROSETTE. When you have completed the circle of pleats, trim any excess from the end of the last pleat. Tuck the end of the last pleat under the edge of the first pleat, and hot glue an accent piece in the center.

ATTACH THE ROSETTE. To attach the rosette to a project, simply peel the paper backing from the bottom circle and press the rosette onto your project piece.

CHAPTER 1:

Roll out the Fashion

You might be thinking tape and fashion don't mix, but *duct* tape and fashion are actually a perfect pair. Duct tape's durability allows it to withstand almost anything life throws at it, from a day at school to a movie night with friends. And unlike fabric, duct tape is waterproof, making it easy to clean and difficult to ruin in an unexpected rain shower (unlike the suede boots that might be living in your closet). If that wasn't enough to convince you, consider that if you manage to do some damage to a duct tape piece, it's completely repairable (the suede boats, not so much). You can always remake or refurbish a project that has begun to wear— and the second time around, you might decide to change the pattern or include some additional embellishments.

All of these things are reason enough to introduce duct tape into your wardrobe, but the ultimate reason for delving into duct tape fashion is—it's fun! Duct tape comes in tons of bright colors and patterns, in rolls and in sheets. Exploring the myriad of color combinations and discovering a favorite pattern makes working with duct tape a blast! So instead of pondering whether you can really get on board with duct tape fashion, just grab a roll of tape and start crafting. Before you know it, you'll have a finished, wearable item in your hands and you'll never look back. In fact, you'll be thinking, what should I make next…

Kilt, page 62

Bow Choker

Talk about simplicity, this cute choker can be made in minutes using two of the building blocks from the Getting Started section: the folded thin strip (page 14) and the bow (page 15). Once you see how easy it is, you'll want to make one to coordinate with every outfit!

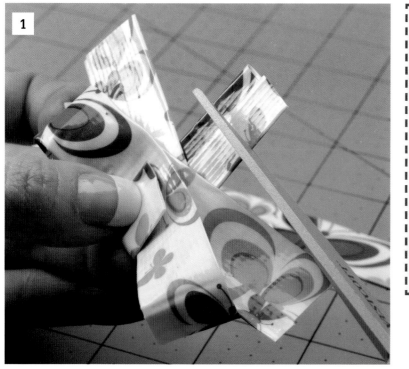

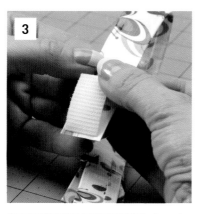

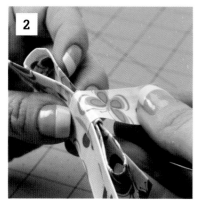

Tools and Materials

- ❏ Duct Tape:
  - 1 Butterfly Roll (choker)
- ❏ Nonstick Scissors
- ❏ Cork-Backed Ruler
- ❏ Flexible Tape Measure
- ❏ Hook-and-Loop Fastener Strips with Adhesive Backing
- ❏ Cutting Mat (optional)

MAKE THE STRAP AND BOW. Measure the circumference of your neck and add 1½" (38mm). Cut a strip of duct tape to that length from a roll. Make a folded thin strip using the method described on page 14. Then, make a bow using the method described on page 15. You can make the bow out of the same color or pattern of duct tape you used for the strap, or use a different color or pattern.

ATTACH THE BOW. Place the bow on the strap where you desire, and secure it by wrapping a piece of duct tape around the bow and the strap.

ATTACH THE FASTENERS. Attach hook-and-loop fastener strips to each end of the strap. Attach the hook piece to the front side, and the loop piece to the back side.

ADHESIVE ADVICE

When attaching hook-and-loop fasteners to wearable items, make sure you position the fasteners so the hook side points away from your body. This saves your skin from irritation!

T-shirt Sleeve Bunchers

These sleeve bunchers add some fun styling to an oversized T-shirt. Use them to hold up your sleeves, or even attach one to the front of your shirt to show off your midriff. And don't miss the cool sidebar on page 36, which tells you how to make a buncher to tighten up the body of a shirt. Make sleeve bunchers in the colors of your favorite sports team and wear them with a jersey, or make them to match your favorite T-shirt. Accent them with any type of embellishment you desire, from buttons, to gems, to stickers, to rosettes. There's no end to the possibilities!

Tools and Materials

❑ Duct Tape:

    • 1 Checker Roll (bunchers)

❑ Gemstones or Novelty Buttons

❑ Hook-and-Loop Fastener Strips with Adhesive Backing

❑ Nonstick Scissors

❑ Cork-Backed Ruler

❑ Hot Glue Gun

❑ Glue Sticks

❑ Cutting Mat (optional)

MAKE THE STRAP AND ATTACH THE FASTENERS. Create a 12" (305mm)-long folded thin strip using the method described on page 14. Then, measure and cut 3¾" (95mm)-long hook-and-loop fastener strips. Attach the fasteners to each end of the strip, placing the hook piece on the front side and the loop piece on the back side.

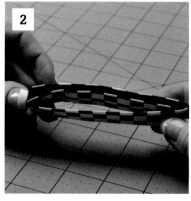

FOLD THE BUNCHER. Crease the folded thin strip where it meets the hook-and-loop fasteners, and close the buncher.

EMBELLISH. Attach gems, stickers, buttons, rosettes, or any other embellishments desired to the top of the buncher. Repeat these steps to make a matching buncher for your other sleeve.

ADHESIVE ADVICE

When positioning hook-and-loop fasteners on wearable items, it is helpful to secure one fastener piece in place on the project as a guide, and then lay the corresponding fastener piece on top of it with the adhesive side exposed. When you close the item, the fastener piece with the sticky side exposed will attach in just the right place for a perfect fit.

Petal Bracelets

Put together a string of petal points and you have a petal bracelet. I like to make my bracelets by alternating petal points in different patterns and colors, but you can choose to use the same color or pattern throughout. Try making a set of petal point bracelets in coordinating colors and wear them like a set of bangles. These also make great party favors! Petal point bracelets require a lot of petal points. See steps 1–3 for a great method for making lots of petal points quickly and easily.

MEASURE AND CUT THE PETAL POINT SEGMENTS. You will need about 24–30 petal points for each bracelet. To create multiple petal points quickly, place several 12" (305mm)-long strips of duct tape parallel to each other on a cutting mat. Using a hobby knife and ruler, measure and cut the strips into 3" (76mm)-long segments.

FORM THE PETAL POINTS. Create a petal point from each 3" (76mm) segment by folding one corner down along the edge of the strip, and then folding the opposite corner down along the opposite edge to form a point (see page 13).

Tools and Materials

- ❑ Duct Tape:
  - 1 Digital Camo Roll (bracelet)
  - 1 Neon Pink Roll (bracelet)
- ❑ Nonstick Scissors
- ❑ Hobby Knife
- ❑ Cutting Mat
- ❑ Cork-Backed Ruler
- ❑ Hot Glue Gun
- ❑ Glue Sticks

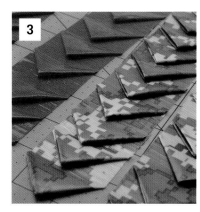

TEMPORARILY PLACE THE PETAL POINTS. Once you have completed a petal point, stick it to your cutting mat until you are ready to use it. Keep your finished petal points in neat rows so you can easily pick them up and use them to create your bracelet.

FOLD IN THE EDGES. Take one petal point and flip it over so the sticky side is exposed. Fold the edges into the middle, forming a flattened tube with a pointed tip. The back end of the petal point should be slightly tapered.

ADD A SECOND PETAL POINT. Attach a second petal point to the first so that the pointed tips align to create a chevron shape. Fold the edges of the second petal point into the middle as you did previously, wrapping them around the first point.

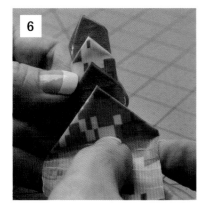

6

FINISH THE LENGTH OF THE BRACELET. Continue adding petal points to the bracelet until it is the length you desire.

7

TRIM. Trim the excess from the last petal point you added, leaving a tail long enough to be inserted into the opening in the first petal point.

8

SHAPE THE TAIL. Squeeze the tail of the last petal point to give it a round shape.

ADHESIVE ADVICE

Keep the tension on the bracelet consistent as you work so that the folded points have an even width.

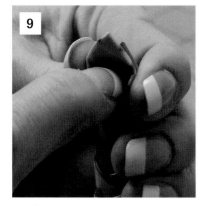

9

OPEN THE FIRST PETAL POINT. Use your finger to widen the opening of the first petal point.

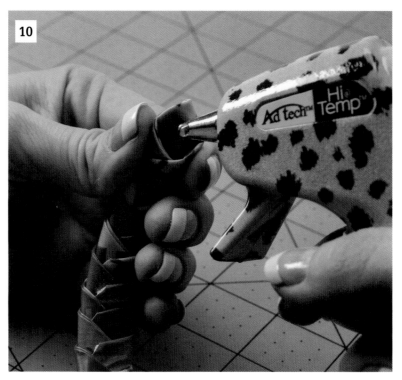

10

FINISH THE BRACELET. Test the fit of the bracelet before gluing and make any necessary adjustments. When you're happy with the fit, fill the opening of the first petal point halfway full with hot glue and insert the tail of the last petal point.

Suspenders

Bring suspenders into the twenty-first century with a vibrant pattern and well-placed embellishments. This is the kind of project you can play up or play down according to your taste. Use neon colors and a heap of embellishments to create suspenders that can be paired with a costume for a party, or use a more subdued pattern with some subtle accent pieces for everyday wear.

Tools and Materials

- ❑ Duct Tape:
  - 1 Argyle Roll (suspenders and rosettes)
  - 1 Denim Roll (suspenders and rosettes)
  - 1 Gold Roll (rosettes)
- ❑ Suspender Clips
- ❑ Cover Button Kit (rosette accent pieces)
- ❑ Nonstick Scissors
- ❑ Cork-Backed Ruler
- ❑ Flexible Tape Measure
- ❑ Compass (optional)
- ❑ Hot Glue Gun
- ❑ Glue Sticks
- ❑ Cutting Mat (optional)

1 MEASURE AND CREATE THE STRAPS. Measure from the front of your waist, over your shoulder, to the back of your waist. Add 3½" (89mm). Measure and trim a piece of duct tape of that length from a roll and fold it into a folded thin strip (see page 14). Repeat to make the second suspender strap.

ADHESIVE ADVICE

If you are not comfortable working with a long strip of tape to make the strap, use several smaller strips and piece them together to make a strap of the appropriate length.

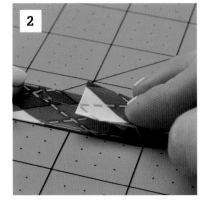

FOLD THE END. Take one suspender strap and place it facedown on your work surface. Fold one end of the strap over an inch (25mm).

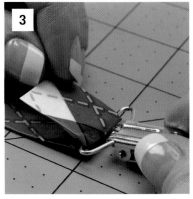

ATTACH A CLIP. Slide a suspender clip over the end of the strap, placing it in the fold you made previously. Make sure the clip is facedown like the strap.

ADHESIVE ADVICE

Use the same method you did to make the suspenders to create a clip T-shirt buncher, which can be used to tighten the body of a large T-shirt. It's also great for keeping your gloves or mittens nearby.

SECURE THE CLIP. Cut a 1" x 2" (25 x 51mm) piece of tape, place it sticky side up under the end of the strap, and fold the edges over the end of the strap to secure the clip in place. Repeat steps 2–4 to attach clips to the other end of the strap and both ends of the second strap.

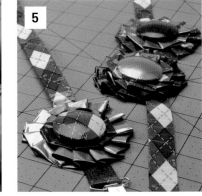

EMBELLISH. Add embellishments, such as layered rosettes (see page 24), to each suspender.

Layered Rosette Bracelet

A layered rosette makes a fun and flirty centerpiece for this bracelet. To create an interchangeable bracelet, make several layered rosettes and attach the loop side of hook-and-loop fasteners to the back of each one. Attach the hook side of the fasteners to the bracelet band. Now you can change the look of your bracelet in an instant to match your mood. Remember that each layered rosette can be fully customized to your taste with your favorite colors, patterns, and accent pieces.

Tools and Materials

- ❏ Duct Tape:
  - 1 Neon Pink Sheet (rosette bases)
  - 1 Zig-Zag Roll (bottom ruffle)
  - 1 Blue Polka Dot Roll (middle ruffle)
  - 1 Neon Yellow Roll (top ruffle)
- ❏ Rosette Accent Piece
- ❏ Nonstick Scissors
- ❏ Cork-Backed Ruler
- ❏ Compass
- ❏ Flexible Tape Measure
- ❏ Hot Glue Gun
- ❏ Glue Sticks
- ❏ Cutting Mat (optional)

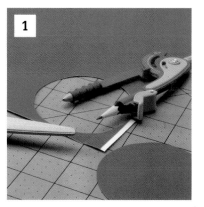

MEASURE AND CUT THE FIRST CIRCLE. This project calls for a three-layer rosette. To start, use a compass to measure and draw a 3" (76mm)-diameter circle on a sheet of duct tape. Cut out the circle.

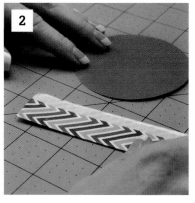

CUT AND FOLD THE FIRST STRIP. Measure and trim a 12" (305mm)-long strip of tape from a roll. Fold the strip lengthwise, leaving a portion of the sticky side exposed along one edge.

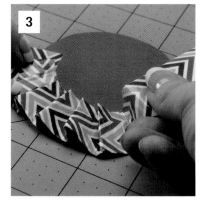

CREATE THE PLEATS. Use the strip to create a row of pleats around the edge of the duct tape sheet circle, following the method described on page 24. If the strip is too short to go all the way around the circle, patch it as needed following the method used to patch a ruffle (page 19). When finished, tuck the end of the last pleat under the edge of the first pleat.

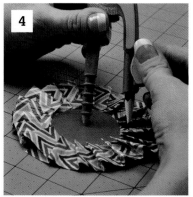

MEASURE AND CUT THE SECOND CIRCLE. Use the compass to determine the size of the second circle. Cut a circle of that size from a sheet of duct tape.

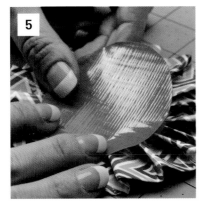

5

ATTACH THE SECOND CIRCLE. Peel away the paper backing and attach the second circle to the rosette, placing it in the center so that it overlaps the edges of the pleats.

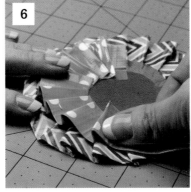

6

CREATE THE SECOND ROW OF PLEATS. Measure and cut a second 12" (305mm)-long strip from a roll of duct tape, fold it, and use it to create a row of pleats around the edge of the second circle. Patch as needed, and finish by tucking the end of the last pleat under the edge of the first pleat.

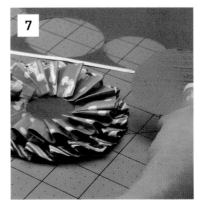

7

MEASURE, CUT, AND ATTACH THE FINAL CIRCLE. Use the compass to determine the size of the final circle. Cut a circle of that size from the sheet of duct tape, and secure it to the rosette.

8

CREATE THE FINAL ROW OF PLEATS. Cut a final 12" (305mm)-long strip of tape from a roll, fold it, and use it to create the last row of pleats around the last circle. Patch as needed.

9

ATTACH A CENTERPIECE. Trim away any excess tape from the end of the final pleat and tuck the end under the edge of the first pleat. Hot glue the object of your choice to the center of the rosette. Set aside to dry.

10

SIZE THE WRISTBAND. The wristband of this bracelet is a wide strip made following the method described on page 16. Measure the circumference of your wrist and add 2" (51mm). Measure and trim two strips of duct tape of that length from a roll.

11

12

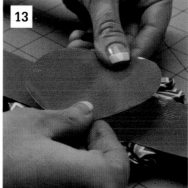

13

MAKE THE WRISTBAND. Place one of the strips sticky side up on your work surface. Attach the second strip to the first so the sticky sides are facing each other. Remember to look down on the strips as you are aligning and attaching them. Trim away any exposed sticky portions from the edges of the finished wide strip.

ATTACH THE ROSETTE. Remove the paper backing from the layered rosette and place it facedown. Attach the wristband to the rosette, making sure it is centered.

COVER THE STICKY BACKING. Cut a circle from a sheet of duct tape that is large enough to cover the bottom of the layered rosette. Remove the paper backing from the circle and use it to cover the exposed sticky portions of tape on the bottom of the layered rosette. Make sure you capture the bracelet's wristband between the circle and the bottom of the layered rosette.

14

ADHESIVE ADVICE

Alter this project to create a headband by making the band long enough to fit around your head. You can even ruffle the side of the band for an extra-flirty look.

ATTACH THE FASTENERS. Attach hook-and-loop fasteners to each end of the bracelet. Remember to position the fasteners so that when the bracelet is worn, the hook side will point away from your skin.

Collar & Cuffs

Looking for a quick and easy way to create an attention-grabbing duct tape prom look? These bold collar and cuffs can add some unique sophistication to a school dance outfit. The details, like the buttons and contrasting piping, make this project extra-special and extra-refined (with a splash of fun, of course). And ladies, don't shy away; these sassy pieces will look fantastic on you, too. The menswear look is all the rage these days! Go with the classic white collar and cuffs, or take a walk on the wild side by incorporating unexpected colors and patterns. Pair them with your favorite tank top for a great casual look.

Tools and Materials

- ❑ Duct Tape:

  - 3 (or more) White Sheets depending on your wrist and neck size (collar and cuffs)

  - 4 (or more) Black Sheets depending on your wrist and neck size (collar and cuffs)

  - 1 Neon Pink Roll (covered buttons)

  - 1 White Roll (seams and patching)

  - 1 Black Roll (seams and patching)

- ❑ Cover Button Kit

- ❑ Hook-and-Loop Fastener Strips with Adhesive Backing

- ❑ Nonstick Scissors

- ❑ Paper Trimmer (optional)

- ❑ Hobby Knife (optional)

- ❑ Cutting Mat (optional)

- ❑ Cork-Backed Ruler

- ❑ Flexible Tape Measure

- ❑ Hot Glue Gun

- ❑ Glue Sticks

The author used these products for the project. Substitute your choice of colors and patterns as desired.

ADHESIVE ADVICE

Use a paper trimmer to quickly and easily cut duct tape sheets to the proper dimensions.

CUFFS

MEASURE AND CUT THE WHITE LAYER. Measure the circumference of your wrist with a tape measure and add 3½" (89mm). Trim a sheet of white duct tape to that length and 6½" (165mm) wide. If necessary, patch sheets of duct tape together to reach the necessary length.

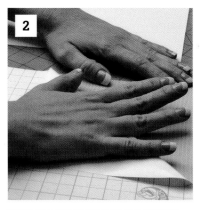

REMOVE THE PAPER BACKING. Peel the paper backing from a full-size sheet of black duct tape by placing the sheet facedown and removing the paper backing slowly, keeping it as flat as possible.

ATTACH THE LAYERS. Take the white sheet (with the paper backing still on) and attach it, color side up, to the black sheet as shown.

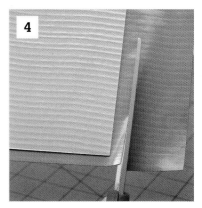

TRIM. Trim away any excess tape as needed to create an even border around all sides of the white sheet.

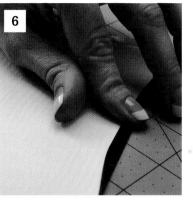

NOTCH THE CORNERS. Use a hobby knife or scissors to cut square notches from all four corners of the black sheet.

FOLD OVER THE EDGES. Fold the edges of the black sheet up over the edges of the white sheet, starting in the middle of a side and working your way out to the corners. The end result should be something that looks like the piping on a tuxedo.

FOLD THE CUFF. Fold the cuff in half lengthwise, so the black side is on the inside and the white side with the piping is on the outside.

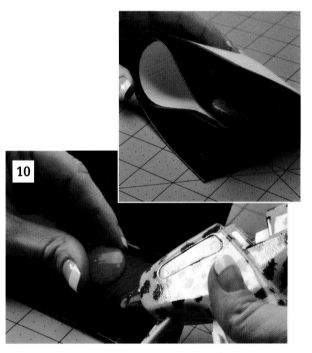

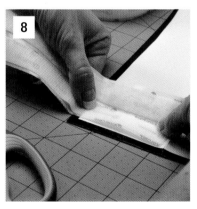

CUT THE FASTENERS TO SIZE. Cut hook-and-loop fastener strips to fit the width of the cuff.

ATTACH THE FASTENERS. Attach hook-and-loop fastener strips to each end of the cuff, positioning them so that they meet when you pinch the cuff closed around your wrist.

MAKE AND ATTACH THE BUTTONS. Make two covered buttons using the method described on page 21. Hot glue the buttons into place, attaching them to the inside corners of the cuff, behind the fasteners. If the button shank prevents you from gluing the button flat, fold it over or trim it off. Repeat to make the second cuff.

COLLAR

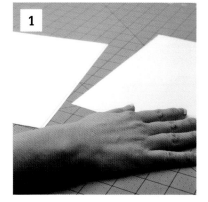

MEASURE THE COLLAR LENGTH.
Measure the circumference of your neck and add 6½" (165mm). This is the length of the collar. Two angled pieces cut from a duct tape sheet and placed end to end, creating a piece about 20" (508mm) long, form the collar. If a larger collar is needed, patch two sheets of duct tape together before proceeding to the next step.

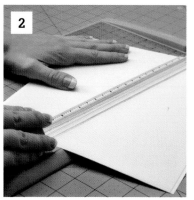

CUT THE WHITE LAYER. Cut a sheet of white duct tape lengthwise at an angle. To do this, I placed about 5" (127mm) of the top of the sheet to the left side of the trimmer blade and about 3" (76mm) to the right. For the bottom, I placed about 5" (127mm) of the sheet to the right of the trimmer blade and about 3" (76mm) to the left.

CONNECT THE PIECES. Place the angled pieces face up on your work surface with the small ends together. Use a strip cut from a roll of white duct tape to connect the pieces.

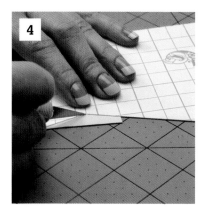

TRIM THE CONNECTING STRIP.
Using a hobby knife, cut away any portion of the connecting strip that extends past the edges of the collar.

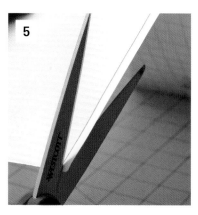

TRIM THE PAPER. Trim away any portion of the paper backing that extends past the tape.

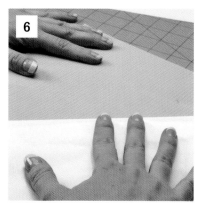

PREPARE THE BACK LAYER.
Remove the paper backing from a full-size sheet of black duct tape.

ADHESIVE ADVICE

To save scraps of duct tape for a later project, keep the paper backing you've removed from a sheet of duct tape and attach scraps to it for future use. You can also use the paper backing to easily cut small shapes from strips trimmed from a duct tape roll.

ATTACH ONE SIDE. With the black sheet sticky side up on your work surface, take the collar, with the paper backing still on, and position it over the black sheet. Attach the collar, color side up, to the black sheet.

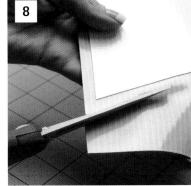

TRIM. Cut away any excess portions of the black tape as needed to create an even border around all sides of the collar. Keep the scraps if desired for a future project.

ATTACH THE OTHER SIDE. Remove the paper backing from another full-size sheet of black duct tape and attach the other side of the collar, color side up, to it. Trim away any excess portions of the black sheet to create an even border.

PATCH THE CENTER. Add a piece of black tape to the back of the collar to connect the black sheets. Trim away any excess with a hobby knife.

NOTCH THE CORNERS. Cut square notches in the four corners of the collar as you did for the cuffs.

NOTCH THE CENTER ANGLE. Cut two straight lines on each side of the center angle of the collar, and a line extending directly from the angle.

FOLD OVER THE EDGES. Fold the edges of the black sheet over the sides of the collar, starting in the middle and working toward the corners. Trim away any excess tape at the corners as necessary.

PATCH AS NEEDED. If any white areas are exposed, such as in the center angle, patch them with small pieces of black tape.

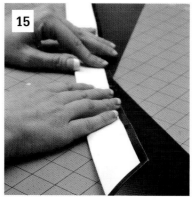

FOLD DOWN THE EDGE. Fold the long, straight edge of the collar down lengthwise so that the black sides are together and the edge meets the center angle.

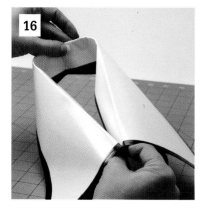

MAKE THE COLLAR SHAPE. Fold the project into the proper collar shape to determine where to attach the fasteners.

ATTACH THE FASTENERS. Attach hook-and-loop fasteners to the inside ends of the collar.

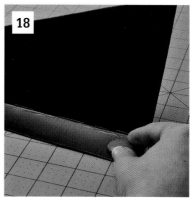

MAKE AND ATTACH THE BUTTONS. Make two covered buttons and hot glue them in place on both ends of the collar.

Keychain

Keychains are the perfect way to accessorize your purse or backpack, and this keychain project can be made in any shape you want, from a cutesy heart to a mod geometric square to a freeform cloud with a flaming lightning bolt. Do you play sports? Make a keychain in the shape of a soccer ball or volleyball. Do you play in the band? I see a music note keychain in your future. Part of the drama club? Make a keychain in the shape of the commedia masks, decorating one side as happy and the other as sad. Car-shaped keychains make great sweet sixteen gifts! This project can be customized to fit your personal taste, style, and interests.

Tools and Materials

- ❑ Duct Tape:
  - • 1 Neon Pink Sheet (keychain layers)
  - • 1 Purple Sheet (layered sticker)
  - • 1 Mustache Roll (keychain strap)
  - • 1 Electric Blue Roll (rosette)
  - • 1 Peace Sign Roll (keychain accent)
  - • 1 Gold Roll (layered sticker)
  - • 1 Checker Roll (layered sticker)
- ❑ Polyurethane Foam (½" [13mm]-thick)
- ❑ Keyring
- ❑ Embellishments (buttons, gemstones, etc.)
- ❑ Nonstick Scissors
- ❑ Hobby Knife
- ❑ Cutting Mat
- ❑ Cork-Backed Ruler
- ❑ Hot Glue Gun
- ❑ Glue Sticks

CUT OUT THE SHAPES. Cut a shape of the desired size from a sheet of duct tape. Then, cut a second shape ½" (13mm) larger on all sides. I chose to make a heart-shaped keychain.

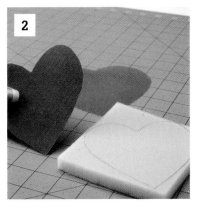

TRACE THE SMALL SHAPE. Trace the outline of the smaller shape on a piece of ½" (13mm)-thick polyurethane foam.

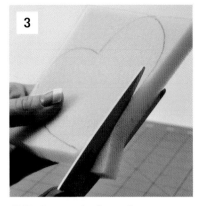

CUT. Cut out the foam shape.

ADHESIVE ADVICE

To ensure the foam shape will be the proper size, cut inside the line you drew.

MAKE THE STRAP AND ATTACH A KEYRING. Measure and trim a 7" (178mm)-long piece of tape from a roll. Form the tape into a folded thin strip using the method described on page 14. Slide a keyring onto the strap and fold the strap in half, positioning the keyring in the fold.

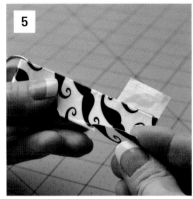

SECURE THE STRAP. Wrap a small piece of tape around the ends of the strap to secure it.

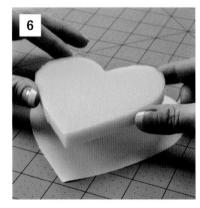

ATTACH THE FOAM. Remove the paper backing from the large keychain shape and place it sticky side up on your work surface. Place the foam piece in the center of the tape.

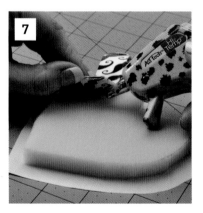

ATTACH THE STRAP. Secure the strap to the foam with a bit of hot glue. You can place the strap directly at the top of the shape or off to one side as I did.

NOTCH THE TAPE. Using a hobby knife, cut notches ½" (13mm) apart in the exposed border of tape surrounding the foam.

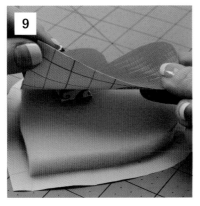

PLACE THE TOP LAYER. Place the small shape, with the paper backing still on, on top of the foam.

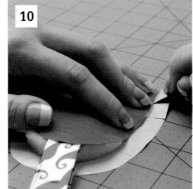

FOLD OVER THE EDGES. Fold the notched pieces of tape up over the small shape to hold it in place, pressing down on the edges of the foam as you work. Wait to fold up the notched portions of tape located beneath the strap until later.

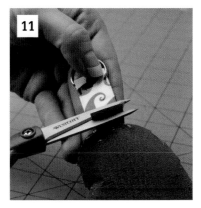

TRIM THE REMAINING TAPE. Shorten the notched piece of tape located under the strap.

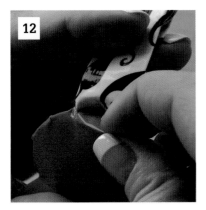

TUCK IN THE TAPE. Fold the notched piece up and tuck the edge against the strap, pushing it into the center of the keychain.

SECURE THE TAPE. Close the opening in the keychain by placing a drop of hot glue between the tape and the strap.

EMBELLISH. Embellish the keychain as desired. I used a rosette with a button center, a gemstone, a duct tape sticker, and a patterned piece of tape.

Purse

If you're like me, your purse goes with you everywhere, and it can get worn pretty quickly. A duct tape purse, however, can withstand any marathon shopping session, dinner gathering, or fall from the front seat of the car. This project makes use of an "upcycled" plastic grocery bag, something you likely have on hand already. You can also scale this project up with a larger plastic bag, like those used by department stores, to make a beach bag. And the great thing is, if you tend to overstuff your bag to the point that it breaks, you can simply fix it by adding more duct tape!

DETERMINE THE SIZE. For this project, you will use a cardboard box to shape the purse and a plastic bag as the liner. Select a box of the size and shape you desire and a plastic bag large enough to hold it.

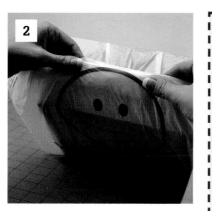

FIT THE BOX IN THE BAG. Turn the bag inside out so that any patterns or text on it will be facing the inside of your purse when the project is completed. Place the box in the bag. Then, roll the handles and top of the bag down tightly against the top of the box. Secure with clear packaging tape.

Tools and Materials

- ❑ Duct Tape:
  - • 2 (or more) Digital Camo Sheets depending on the desired size of the purse (purse front and back)
  - • 1 Argyle Roll (purse sides, bottom, and straps)
- ❑ Cardboard Box (purse form)
- ❑ Plastic Bag
- ❑ 4 Plastic Curtain Grommets
- ❑ Marker
- ❑ Clear Packaging Tape
- ❑ Nonstick Scissors
- ❑ Cork-Backed Ruler
- ❑ Cutting Mat (optional)

TRIM THE SIDES. Trim away the excess plastic from the bag along the sides of the box.

SECURE THE SIDES. Pull the edges of the plastic bag together along the sides of the box and secure with clear packaging tape. The final result will be the box wrapped snugly in the bag with as few wrinkles and bunches as possible.

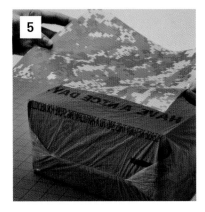

COVER THE SIDES. Remove the paper backing from a sheet of duct tape and use it to cover the front of the box-in-bag assembly.

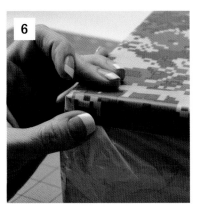

FOLD OVER THE EDGES. Fold the edges of the sheet over the bottom and sides of the assembly, but not over the top. To cover the corners, crease the tape like you would when wrapping a present, tucking the side edge of the tape under the bottom edge.

TRIM. Trim away any excess tape along the top edge of the assembly. Use a second sheet of tape to cover the back in the same manner.

BEGIN WRAPPING THE SIDES AND BOTTOM. Take a roll of duct tape, unroll some tape, and secure it along the left edge of one of the sides of the assembly.

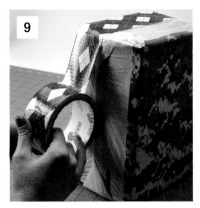

CONTINUE WRAPPING. Continue unrolling tape and securing it to the assembly, wrapping it down one side, across the bottom, and up the other side. Keep the tape taut as you work.

WRAP THE RIGHT EDGE. Repeat the wrapping process, this time placing the tape along the right edge of the side of the assembly, wrapping it down the side, across the bottom, and up the other side.

ADHESIVE ADVICE

Using patterned tape along the side and bottom of the purse makes the transition between strips less noticeable.

FINISH WRAPPING. Use a third and final strip to cover the exposed middle portion along the sides and bottom.

TRIM THE TOP. Trim away the bag from the top of the box, leaving a little extra along the edges.

REMOVE THE BOX. Remove the box from the purse by pushing on the bottom with your thumbs while holding the sides of the purse with your fingers. Then, pull the box from the purse.

ADHESIVE ADVICE

To create a sturdy bottom for your purse, cut a piece of cardboard to fit the bottom, cover it with duct tape, and place it in your purse.

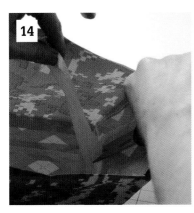

TRIM THE PLASTIC. Cut away any excess pieces of plastic from the inside of the purse. If desired, turn the purse inside out to help with this process.

TRIM THE TOP. Trim the tape around the top of the purse to make clean, straight edges. You may use a ruler to draw lines along the top edges if you prefer that method to cutting the straight line freehand.

MARK THE HOLES. Select an area near the corner of the purse where you would like to place the end of a handle. Trace the grommet template using a marker. Measure how far the marking is from the top and side of the purse and use that measurement to place and trace the template at the remaining three corners.

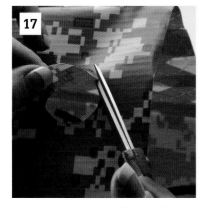

CUT THE HOLES. Following the circles you drew previously, cut out the four holes for the grommets.

PLACE THE GROMMETS. Place a grommet bottom inside the purse, aligning it with one of the holes you've made. Push the grommet bottom through the hole and snap the grommet top in place. Repeat with the remaining three grommets.

MAKE AND ATTACH THE HANDLES. The handles for the purse are made from a single continuous folded thin strip that is threaded through all four grommets. Make a folded thin strip of the length you desire for the handles, using the method described on page 14. Slip one end of the strip, from the outside of the purse, through a grommet and through the one directly opposite it. Slip the other end of the strip through the remaining two grommets.

SECURE THE HANDLES. Overlap the ends of the handles and secure them with a piece of duct tape.

Leg Warmers

I love matching leg warmers with my favorite pair of black boots, and with '80s styling making a comeback in today's fashion scene, this project is right on trend. I used winter-themed duct tape as the border for the outside of my leg warmers and flame-patterned duct tape as the trim for the lining side, giving these leg warmers a mix of "hot" and "cold." You can mimic my pattern choices or alter them to fit your taste. Maybe you love summer and want your leg warmers to have a tropical look to remind you of warm weather when it's cold outside. Or perhaps you'd like to go all out with red and green duct tape to create a holiday set of leg warmers. No matter what your style is, there's definitely a duct tape option for you!

Tools and Materials

- ❏ Duct Tape:
  - • 2 (or more) Zig-Zag Zebra™ Sheets depending on your foot size (legwarmers, outside)
  - • 2 (or more) Totally Tie-Dye™ Sheets depending on your foot size (legwarmers, liner)
  - • 1 Electric Blue Sheet (outside trim and ruffle)
  - • 1 Flames Roll (liner border)
  - • 1 Penguin Roll (outside border)
  - • 1 Chrome Roll (ruffle)
- ❏ Hook-and-Loop Fastener Strips with Adhesive Backing
- ❏ Nonstick Scissors
- ❏ Cork-Backed Ruler
- ❏ Flexible Tape Measure
- ❏ Cutting Mat (optional)

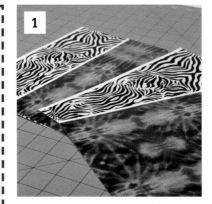

MEASURE AND SELECT THE MATERIALS. Point your toe downward and measure around the back of your heel to the front of your foot. The leg warmers need a circumference slightly larger than this measurement to fit over your feet. Select four full-size sheets of duct tape, two in one pattern or color for the outside, and two in another for the lining.

ATTACH THE SHEETS. Take the two outside sheets and remove the paper backing. Attach the two sheets lengthwise by overlapping the edges. Measure the length of the large sheet. If it is smaller than the measurement you took of the circumference of you foot, attach a third sheet to reach the necessary measurement.

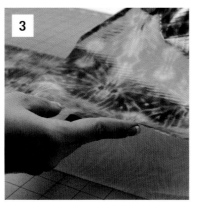

ATTACH THE REMAINING SHEETS. Remove the paper backing from a liner sheet and attach it, sticky side down, to the large sheet you created previously. Repeat with the remaining liner sheet. The end result should be an extra-large, double-sided sheet of duct tape. Trim away any exposed sticky portions of tape from the edges.

ATTACH BORDERS TO THE LINING. Add borders to the liner side of your leg warmer by unrolling lengths of tape and attaching them to the long edges of the liner side of the sheet. Trim away any excess.

ADHESIVE ADVICE

When attaching two sheets of duct tape to each other (sticky sides together), place one sheet sticky side up on your work surface and lower a second sheet onto it. Hold the sheet you are lowering so that it forms a U. Attach the center portion of the sheet first, and then slowly lower the other portions to avoid wrinkles.

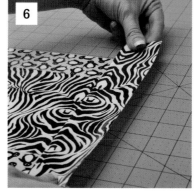

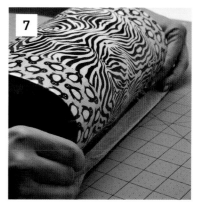

ATTACH BORDERS TO THE OUTSIDE. Flip the sheet over and attach borders to the outside of the legwarmer.

TAPE THE EDGE. Using a roll of tape that matches the pattern of the outside of the leg warmer, unroll a piece the length of the short edge of the sheet. Attach the tape to the edge of the sheet, placing half the strip on the sheet and allowing half of it to extend past the edge. Trim away any excess along the top and bottom.

FORM A TUBE. Bring the ends of the sheet together to form a tube, and secure them with the strip of tape.

PATCH THE BORDERS. Patch the borders along the seam by adding small pieces of tape.

SIZE AND FOLD. Put the leg warmer on and pinch the excess material until it fits as tightly around your leg as you wish, making note of the size. Then, remove the tube and fold it as shown, creating two creases. During the next step, you will attach hook-and-loop fastener strips along these creases. This allows you to slip the legwarmer over your heel, and then tighten it around your leg, using the hook-and-loop fasteners to hold it in place.

ATTACH THE FASTENERS. Cut hook-and-loop fastener strips that measure the length of the tube. Attach the hook piece to the leg warmer, aligning the top edge of the piece with the upper crease. Attach the loop piece near the bottom crease. Make sure the fasteners will connect when the leg warmer is folded closed.

ADD TRIM TO THE BOTTOM. Create trim for the bottom of the leg warmer by cutting a thin strip of tape from a sheet (about the width of a row of squares) and attaching it to the bottom edge of the leg warmer.

ADD TRIM TO THE TOP. Embellish the top of the leg warmer by adding a ruffle using the method described on page 17.

SECURE THE RUFFLE. Secure the edge of the ruffle using the same color tape you used to trim the bottom of the leg warmer.

MAKE THE SECOND LEG WARMER. To wear the leg warmer, slide it over your foot and secure it using the fasteners. Repeat to make the second leg warmer.

Fingerless Gloves

Use these gloves to add a pop of color to your winter wardrobe. The fingerless design leaves your digits free to zip your jacket, answer a text, or flip through a book with ease. Make a pair to match a set of duct tape leg warmers (see page 55), or pick colors and patterns that coordinate with your favorite winter coat or hat. And of course, when it comes to adding embellishments, you are only limited by your imagination.

Tools and Materials

❑ Duct Tape:

- 2 (or more) Zig-Zag Zebra™ Sheets depending on your wrist size (gloves, outside)

- 2 (or more) White Sheets depending on your wrist size (gloves, liner)

- 1 Neon Pink Sheet (ruffle)

- 1 Skulls Roll (liner border)

- 1 Zig-Zag Zebra™ Roll (gloves, seam)

- 1 Chrome Roll (ruffle)

- 1 Neon Yellow Roll (bow)

❑ Nonstick Scissors

❑ Paper Trimmer (optional)

❑ Cork-Backed Ruler

❑ Flexible Tape Measure

❑ Hot Glue Gun

❑ Glue Sticks

❑ Cutting Mat (optional)

1 MEASURE AND SELECT THE MATERIALS. Cup your hand as you would when putting on gloves or mittens. Measure around the widest part of your hand. Select four sheets of duct tape, two in one pattern for the outside of the gloves, and two in another pattern for the lining of the gloves.

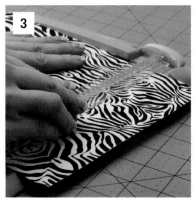

ATTACH THE SHEETS. Attach each liner sheet to an outside sheet of duct tape, placing them with the sticky sides together. The end result is two double-sided sheets of tape.

TRIM THE SHEETS. Trim the sheets to the length you want your gloves to be and to a width that matches the measurement you took during Step 1. Save any excess for future projects.

FOLD THE EDGE. Fold the long edge of one sheet over ½" (13mm).

SECURE THE EDGE. Measure and trim a strip of tape the width of the sheet from a roll. Use it to secure the fold at the edge of the sheet. This tape will be visible later, so select a pattern or color you like. Trim away any excess.

CUT A HOLE FOR THE THUMB. Place your hand on the sheet and determine where you would like to cut the thumb hole. The higher you place the hole, the smaller the section of glove covering your fingers will be. Mark the placement and cut a 1½" (38mm)- diameter hole.

FORM A TUBE. Pull the edges of the sheet together to form a tube and secure them with a strip of tape. Trim away any excess along the top and bottom.

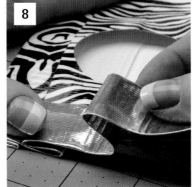

EMBELLISH THE TOP. Embellish the edge of the glove that will be closest to your fingers. I added a ruffle, but you could add a strip of colored tape, a row of gemstones, or any other decorative elements you like.

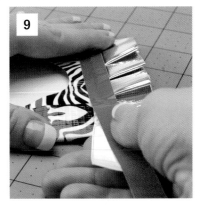

SECURE THE RUFFLE. If you added a ruffle, remember to secure it with a strip of tape cut from a sheet, removing the paper backing as you work.

FOLD THE BOTTOM. Roll the wrist end of the glove up two times to form a cuff. This should expose the strip of tape used to secure the sheet's edge in Step 5.

DISTRESS THE GLOVE. Crumple all the areas of the glove except the embellishments that will be closest to your fingers to make the tape more flexible and give it a distressed look.

EMBELLISH. Try on the glove and determine where you would like to add embellishments. I decided to add a bow, but you could add stickers, gemstones, rosettes, or other items. Secure the embellishments in place with hot glue.

 **IMPORTANT**

Applying hot glue to the glove while wearing it can be dangerous. To avoid burns, remove the glove before adding embellishments. Repeat with the remaining double-sided sheet to make the second glove.

Kilt

This is my modern duct tape interpretation of a traditional Scottish kilt, complete with the customary sporran (the pocket attached to the waistband). While traditional kilts are made of fabric with a tartan pattern, the patterns on the duct tape strips of this kilt give it an updated punk rock vibe. With such a wide variety of duct tape patterns available, this statement piece can be customized to your unique fashion sensibility! You can make it wild and funky or sweet and serene. Feel free to make your kilt express your individual sense of style!

1 TAKE THE MEASUREMENTS. Measure the diameter of your waist and add 3" (76mm). This is the measurement for the waistband of the kilt. Divide the waistband measurement by two. This is the number of strips you will need to make for the kilt.

MAKE THE STRIPS. Measure from your waist to your knee, and make the necessary number of strips this length. To create the strips, measure and cut two pieces of tape from rolls and attach them, sticky sides together, using the method described on page 16.

ALIGN THE STRIPS. Place the strips parallel to each other on your work surface. Make sure the top ends of the strips are even with one another.

CONNECT THE STRIPS. Unroll a piece of tape roll long enough to stretch across all the strips. Secure the tape along the top edge of the strips, making sure half of it extends past the strip ends. It is ok if the tape does not form a straight line; it will be covered in the finished piece.

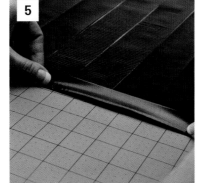

FOLD OVER THE EDGE. Flip the strips over and fold the tape along the top edge of the strips down onto the backs of the strips.

Tools and Materials

❑   Duct Tape:

- 3 Purple Sheets (pocket)

- 3 Flames Sheets (pocket)

- 1 Electric Blue Sheet (pocket ruffle)

- 1 Skulls Roll (kilt strips)

- 1 Pink Zebra Roll (kilt strips, pocket ruffle, and outside waistband)

- 1 Gold Roll (kilt strips)

- 1 Flames Roll (kilt strips)

- 1 Checker Roll (kilt strips)

- 1 Black Roll (kilt strips, pocket ruffle, inner waistband)

❑   Hook-and-Loop Fastener Strips with Adhesive Backing

❑   Nonstick Scissors

❑   Paper Trimmer (optional)

❑   Cork-Backed Ruler

❑   Flexible Tape Measure

❑   Cutting Mat (optional)

ADHESIVE ADVICE

Baby powder is a great way to make duct tape un-sticky. If the adhesive edges of a project become a problem (such as when creating thin fringe), simply dust them with a bit of baby powder to prevent them from unintentionally sticking in unwanted places.

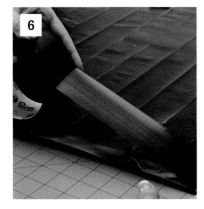

MAKE THE INNER WAISTBAND.
Unroll a length of tape from a roll and place it along the top edge of the back side of the strips. Align the edge of the tape with the tops of the strips.

SELECT THE POCKET PIECES.
Select six sheets of duct tape, three of one color or pattern for the outside of the pocket and three of another color or pattern for the lining.

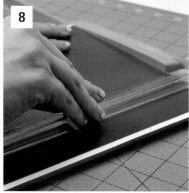

TRIM THE LINER SHEETS. Take two liner sheets and trim them to 7¼" x 8½" (184 x 216mm).

ADHESIVE ADVICE

Save any excess strips or pieces of tape you cut from duct tape sheets and use them for future projects.

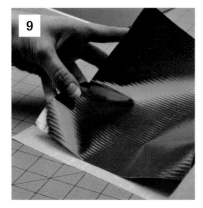

ATTACH A LINER AND OUTER PIECE. Remove the paper backing from an outside sheet. Then, remove the paper backing from one of the liner sheets and attach it to the outside sheet, sticky sides together. Center the liner sheet on the outside sheet. Remember: When attaching sheets of duct tape to one another, work from the center outward.

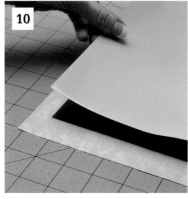

ADD THE SECOND LINER PIECE.
Lay the second liner sheet, sticky side up, on top of the first liner sheet, carefully aligning the edges.

ADD THE SECOND OUTER PIECE.
Remove the paper backing from one of the remaining outside sheets, and attach it, sticky side down, to the other pocket pieces.

SEAL THE POCKET. Run your fingernail along the edge of the liner pieces within the outside pocket pieces to create a tight seal.

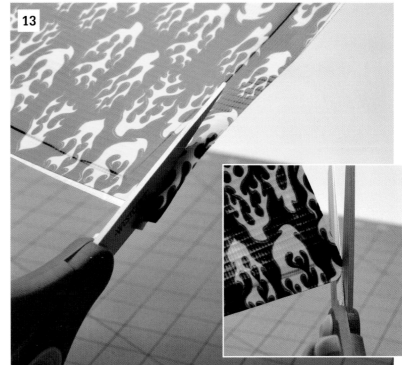

TRIM THE SIDES. Trim the sides and bottom of the pocket, using the liner pieces as a guide, to create a ⅜" (10mm) border around the pocket liner. Then, cut rounded corners at the bottom of the pocket.

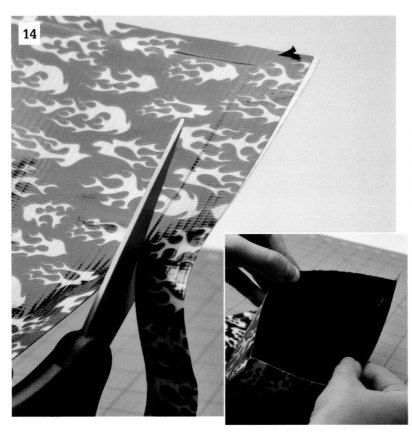

CREATE THE OPENING. Positioning your scissors just below the top of the pocket liner, cut along the top edge of the pocket to create the opening.

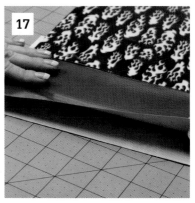

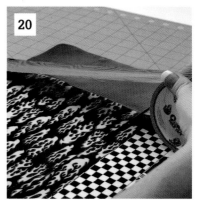

TRIM THE FLAP PIECES. To form the pocket flap, trim the remaining liner and outside sheets to 5¼" x 8¼" (133 x 210mm).

ATTACH THE FRONT FLAP PIECE. Remove the paper backing from the outside sheet and place the top edge of the pocket on top of it, allowing about half the sheet to extend beyond the edge of the pocket.

ATTACH THE BACK FLAP PIECE. Remove the paper backing from the liner sheet, and attach it to the front of the pocket flap, sticky sides together. Align the edge of the liner sheet with the top edge of the pocket. Trim away any excess along the top of the flap.

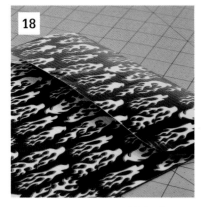

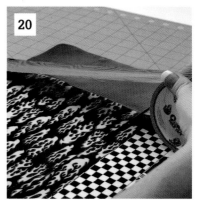

CREASE THE FLAP. Fold the flap over the pocket and crease it along the top edge.

POSITION THE POCKET. Flip the kilt so the outside is facing up. Place the pocket, with the flap open, about one-third the width of the kilt from one of the kilt's ends. Align the top edge of the pocket with the top edge of the waistband.

MAKE THE OUTER WAISTBAND. Unroll a piece of tape long enough to reach across the kilt and attach it along the top edge of the front of the kilt. Align the edge of the tape with the top edge of the kilt. Place the tape OVER the pocket to secure it in place on the kilt.

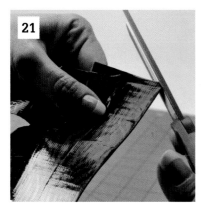

TRIM THE WAISTBAND. Trim any exposed sticky portions of tape from the ends of the waistband.

TRIM THE STRIPS TO SIZE. Hold the kilt against your body and determine how short you'd like to make the strips. Then, trim them to the desired length. You can cut the ends of the strips straight across, at a repeating angle, or at alternating angles as shown.

EMBELLISH THE POCKET FLAP. Close the pocket by folding the flap down. Embellish the pocket flap by adding ruffles, rosettes, gemstones, stickers, or other decorative elements.

ATTACH THE FASTENERS. Attach hook-and-loop fastener strips to the kilt's waistband. Attach the hook piece to the outside of the waistband at one end of the kilt. Attach the loop piece to the inside of the waistband at the other end of the kilt.

Tools and Materials

- ❑ Duct Tape:
  - • 2 White Sheets (cups)
  - • 2 Purple Sheets (cup liners)
  - • 1 Mustache Roll (bottom band and straps)
  - • 1 Neon Pink Roll (bottom band liner, straps liner, and rosettes)
  - • 1 Skulls Roll (ruffle, rosettes, and modesty panel strips)
  - • 1 Neon Yellow Roll (ruffle)
  - • 1 Flames Roll (rosettes and modesty panel strips)
- ❑ Gemstones (rosettes)
- ❑ Button Cover Kit (rosettes)
- ❑ Hook-and-Loop Fastener Strips with Adhesive Backing
- ❑ Nonstick Scissors
- ❑ Cork-Backed Ruler
- ❑ Flexible Tape Measure
- ❑ Compass
- ❑ Hot Glue Gun
- ❑ Glue Sticks
- ❑ Cutting Mat (optional)

Halter Top

Warning: This advanced project is not for the timid duct tape crafter. It's bold, it's colorful, it's fun, and it's got loads of personality. This is the ultimate in extreme duct tape couture! The piece is made of two parts: a bra top, and a removable modesty panel. Wear the modesty panel to take advantage of the flirty fringe. If you're feeling daring, remove the panel to expose your midriff. Strips can be added to tape modesty panel and lengthened to make the piece into a baby doll dress, or you can cut the strips lengthwise to create traditional fringe with lots of movement. No matter how you decide to customize it, this warm-weather wonder will have heads turning wherever you go!

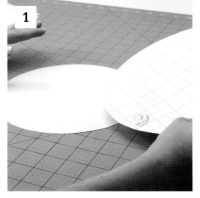

CUT TWO CIRCLES. Measure the diameter of each of your breasts. Then, draw two circles of the same diameters on a sheet of duct tape with a compass. Cut out the circles.

CUT TO THE CENTER. Take each circle and cut straight in from the outer edge until you reach the center point.

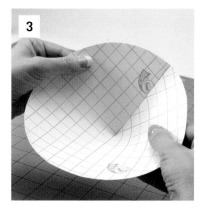

SIZE THE CIRCLES. Hold a circle against your chest and adjust the size by pulling or pushing the cut edges together so they overlap, forming a cup. When you have shaped the circle into the cup size you want, draw a line on the tape along one of the cut edges to indicate the final size. Repeat with the second circle.

CUT AWAY THE PAPER BACKING. Place one of the circles color side up. Peel the tape away from the paper backing up to the line you drew during the previous step. Cut away the exposed portion of the paper backing.

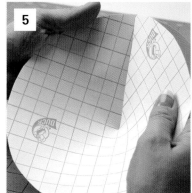

SECURE THE CUP. Reshape the circle into a cup by pulling the cut edges together and overlapping them as before. Use the wedge of tape with the paper backing cut away to hold the cup closed. Repeat steps 4 and 5 to create the second cup.

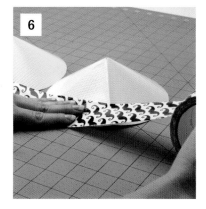

CREATE THE BOTTOM BAND. Measure around your ribcage under your bust and add 3" (76mm). Unroll a piece of tape of that length and secure it to the bottom edge of the front side of each cup, positioning the cups at the center of the length of tape at the appropriate place.

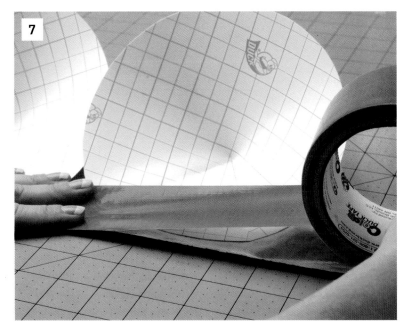

LINE THE BOTTOM BAND. Flip the assembly over and line the bottom band by unrolling a length of duct tape and attaching it to the band, sticky sides together. Make sure you capture the bottom edges of the cups between the two strips of tape. Trim away any exposed sticky portions of tape from the edges.

ATTACH A STRAP. Measure from under your bust to the back of your neck and add 2" (51mm). Unroll a length of tape of that measurement and attach it to the front side of one of the cups, making sure the end of the strap extends down onto the bottom band.

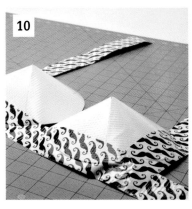

LINE THE STRAP. Flip the assembly over and cover the back of the strap with a matching length of tape, capturing the side edge of the cup between the layers.

CREATE THE SECOND STRAP. Repeat steps 8 and 9 to attach and line the second strap.

ADD THE FIRST RUFFLE. I chose to embellish my top with ruffles and rosettes. To create the top as I did, form a ruffle around the top and sides of each cup.

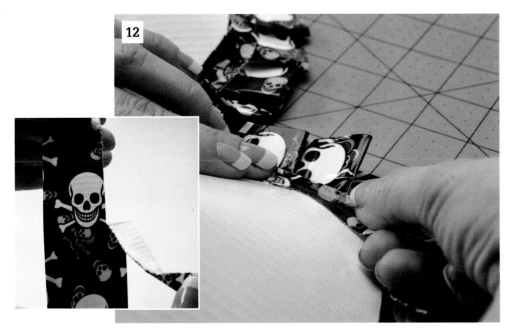

SECURE THE RUFFLE. A fast way to secure the edge of a ruffle that won't be visible in the final piece is to trim a strip of tape from a roll, and then tear the tape lengthwise, removing a small strip as shown. Use this strip to secure the edge of your ruffle in place.

ADD A SECOND RUFFLE. Add a second ruffle, remembering to secure the edge with a strip of tape.

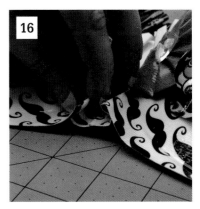

ADD A ROW OF ROSETTES. Glue a row of rosettes along the edge of the second ruffle.

COVER ANY EXPOSED AREAS. Glue rosettes in place to cover any remaining exposed areas on the cups.

TEST THE FIT AND ADJUST. Hold the bra top against your chest to check the fit. If you need to position the cups closer to one another, pinch the portion of the bottom band between the cups together and secure it with a piece of tape.

CUT THE LINER PIECES. To line the cups, draw and cut two circles the same size as the original circles you cut during Step 1. Then, cut a wedge from each circle.

INSERT THE LINER PIECES. Remove the paper backing from one of the liner pieces, and carefully press the piece into the inside of a cup, working from one edge of the wedge to the other. Repeat to line the second cup.

SECURE THE CUPS. Place a strip of tape along the center of the bra top where the two cups meet for extra security.

MAKE THE STRIPS. Create a modesty panel by making wide strips, using the method described on page 16. You can create enough strips to go around the entire bottom band or just enough to cover tape the front portion of the bottom band. You can also cut the fringe vertically into thinner strips for added movement and style!

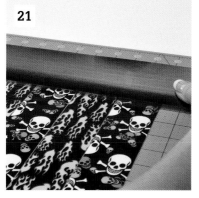

21

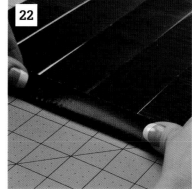

22

23

ATTACH THE STRIPS. Place the strips for the modesty panel parallel to one another, aligning the tops. Unroll a length of duct tape and attach it to the top edges of the strips, making sure about half of the tape extends past the ends of the strips.

FOLD OVER THE EDGE. Flip the strips over and fold the edge of the tape down over the back of the strips to secure them in place.

ATTACH THE HOOK PIECE. Cut hook-and-loop fastener strips that are the width of the modesty panel. Attach the hook piece to the front side of the modesty panel along the top edge.

24

25

ATTACH THE LOOP PIECE. Attach the loop piece to the back side of the bottom band of the bra top. Also cut and attach hook-and-loop fasteners to the end of each of the bra straps. These straps will connect at the back of your neck.

TRIM THE STRIPS. Attach the modesty panel to the bra top and try on the piece. Determine how long you'd like the strips of the modesty panel to be and cut them to the desired length.

CHAPTER 2:
Too Cool for School

Sometimes it can be a challenge to express your creativity and individuality at school. There are classes and assignments to concentrate on, rules to follow, and, many times, a dress code. The projects in this chapter will allow you to freely express your individual personality and style at school—without breaking any rules! A funky pen topper will give you reason to smile while taking that pop quiz in history, and a jazzed up sandwich bag will make an ordinary peanut butter and jelly sandwich seem extraordinary. Looking for something to do during the long bus ride or those occasional moments of free time between classes? Make yourself a duct tape book cover, complete with your favorite board game!

Moms, a personalized pencil case makes a great first day of school gift. And instead of purchasing a new lunch box for your son or daughter this year, why not make a duct tape lunch bag together?

Get busy with your duct tape projects and you can rule the school this year!

Pen Toppers

Pen toppers are a great way to insert some color and flair into your school supplies. They're easy to make, small enough to be unobtrusive in the classroom, and anything but boring. Using a pen with its own fun style will motivate you to take good notes in every class. These fun little pieces also make great gifts or party favors.

FIREWORK FRINGE PEN

Tools and Materials

- ❑ Duct Tape:
  - 1 Spotted Leopard™ Roll (pen wrap and topper)
  - 1 Gold Roll (pen top accent)
  - 1 Zig-Zag Zebra™ Roll (pen top accent)
- ❑ 1 Pen
- ❑ Nonstick Scissors
- ❑ Cork-Backed Ruler
- ❑ Cutting Mat (optional)

MEASURE AND CUT THE TAPE. Measure and trim a strip of tape slightly shorter than the length of your pen from a roll.

WRAP THE PEN. Place the pen along one of the edges of the strip of tape, making sure the tapered portion of the pen extends past the end of the tape. Then, roll the pen to wrap it in the tape, keeping the tapered portion uncovered. Trim any excess from the top.

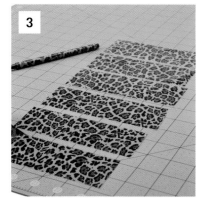

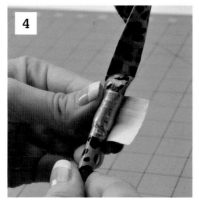

CREATE THE STRIPS. Measure and trim six 6" (152mm)-long strips of tape from a roll. Using the method described on page 16, attach the strips in pairs, sticky sides together, to make three wide strips. Trim away any exposed sticky portions of tape along the edges of the strips.

ATTACH THE FIRST STRIP. Wrap the end of one of the strips around the top of the pen, and secure it with a piece of tape.

ATTACH THE REMAINING STRIPS. Attach the remaining two strips, securing each one to the top of the pen with a piece of tape.

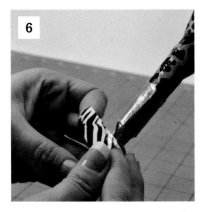

EMBELLISH THE TOP. Use a small strip of tape in a different pattern or color than those used previously to cover the transition area between the tape pieces you used to attach the strips and the pen.

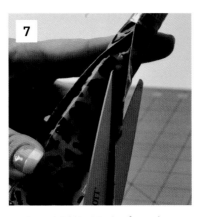

CUT THE FRINGE. Cut from the top of the strips toward the top of the pen to create a fringed tassel.

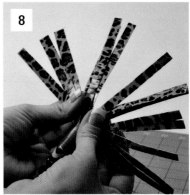

SHAPE THE FRINGE. Spread the fringe pieces out, fluffing them with your fingers to create the shape you desire.

ROSETTE PEN

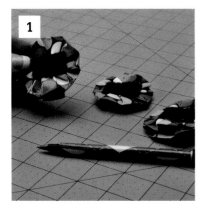

WRAP THE PEN AND MAKE THE ROSETTES. Measure and trim a piece of tape slightly shorter than the length of your pen from a roll. Place the pen at the edge of the tape and roll the pen to wrap it in tape. Then, create three rosettes of your design. Attach hook-and-loop fastener strips to the top of the pen and the rosettes. Attach a hook piece to the pen, and loop pieces to the rosettes.

ATTACH THE ROSETTES. Use the hook-and-loop fasteners to attach the rosettes to the top of the pen. Because the rosettes are interchangeable, you can make as many as you want and place them on the pen (three at a time) as you desire.

Tools and Materials

- ❑ Duct Tape:
  - 1 Argyle Roll (pen wrap)
  - 1 Polka Dot Roll (rosettes)
- ❑ 1 Pen
- ❑ 3 Gemstones (rosettes)
- ❑ Hook-and-Loop Fasteners with Adhesive Backing
- ❑ Nonstick Scissors
- ❑ Cork-Backed Ruler
- ❑ Hot Glue Gun
- ❑ Glue Sticks
- ❑ Cutting Mat (optional)

FLOWER PEN

WRAP THE PEN. Measure and trim a strip of duct tape slightly shorter than the length of your pen from a roll. Place the pen at the edge of the tape and roll it to wrap it in tape.

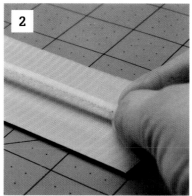

PLACE A CHENILLE STEM. Measure and trim a strip of duct tape slightly longer than a full-length chenille stem from a roll. Place the strip sticky side up on your work surface. Then, take a full-length chenille stem and position it on the center of the tape.

Tools and Materials

- ❑ Duct Tape:
  - • 1 Neon Pink Sheet (pen wrap)
  - • 1 Neon Green Roll (pen wrap and top accent)
  - • 1 Neon Yellow Roll (pen leaves)
  - • 1 Purple Roll (pen leaves)
  - • 1 Checker Roll (pen leaves)
  - • 1 Chrome Roll (pen leaves)
- ❑ 1 Pen
- ❑ 1 Gemstone (flower center)
- ❑ 2 Chenille Stems (leaf centers)
- ❑ Nonstick Scissors
- ❑ Wire Cutters
- ❑ Cork-Backed Ruler
- ❑ Hot Glue Gun
- ❑ Glue Sticks
- ❑ Cutting Mat (optional)

COVER THE STEM. Measure and trim a second strip of tape the same length as the first from a roll. Place it, sticky side down, on top of the chenille stem and first strip of tape. Use a strip of tape in a different color than the first to create a double-sided strip. Trim away any exposed sticky portions of tape along the edges.

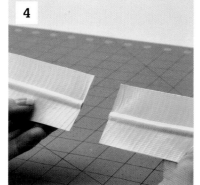

CUT THE STRIP. Using wire cutters, cut the strip with the chenille stem inserted in the middle in half to form two pieces approximately 6" (152mm) long.

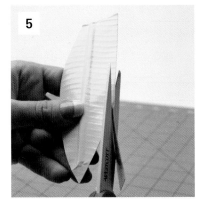

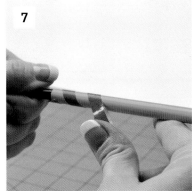

TRIM THE EDGES. Trim the edges of the two strips to create two leaf-like shapes.

CREATE ADDITIONAL LEAVES. Repeat steps 2 through 5 to create two additional leaf shapes.

EMBELLISH THE PEN. Cut a ¼" (6mm)-wide strip of duct tape from a sheet (or use a strip saved from an earlier project) and wrap it diagonally around the pen like the stripe on a candy cane.

ATTACH A LEAF. Cut a 1" (25mm)-wide piece of duct tape from a sheet or roll. Hold a leaf against the top of the pen and attach it with the tape.

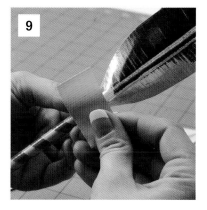

ATTACH THE SECOND LEAF.
Attach a second leaf to the pen top directly opposite the first leaf.

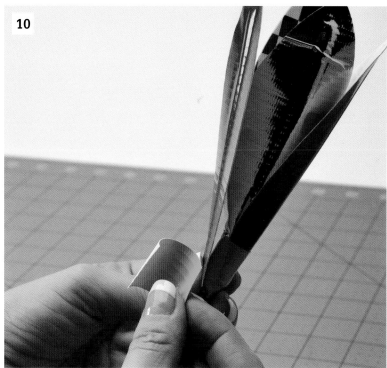

ATTACH THE REMAINING LEAVES. Attach the two remaining leaves to the top of the pen, positioning them opposite one another.

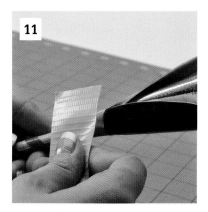

SECURE THE LEAVES. Wrap a 1¼" (32mm)-wide piece of tape around the bases of all four leaves for extra security.

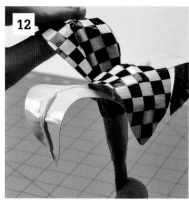

SHAPE THE LEAVES. Fold the leaves down and give them a curved shape. Fluff the leaves until you are satisfied with their appearance.

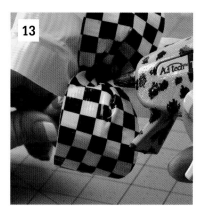

EMBELLISH THE TOP. Hot glue a gem in the center of the leaves.

Sandwich Bag

Let's face it, disposable plastic sandwich bags are pretty…boring. Some have colored seals, and occasionally they are printed with a holiday pattern, but most of them are transparent, colorless, and dull. Not your sandwich bag, though! Armed with a few rolls of duct tape, you can give an ordinary sandwich bag a new look, with plenty of color and interchangeable embellishments. With this new reusable cafeteria accessory, no one will dare call the contents of your lunchbox boring!

CUT AND ATTACH THE FIRST PIECE. Cut a small section of duct tape from a sheet at an angle. Peel off the paper backing and attach the sheet to your sandwich bag, aligning the straight edge of the sheet with the edge of the bag's seal. Trim any excess tape that extends past the sides of the bag.

ATTACH THE FIRST STRIP. Unroll a strip of duct tape slightly longer than the width of the bag and attach it to the bag, allowing the edge of the strip to overlap the first piece by about ⅛" (3mm). Use the angle of the first piece as a guide to place the second piece at the appropriate angle.

Tools and Materials

- ❑ Duct Tape:
  - 1 Neon Pink Sheet (bag cover and layered stickers)
  - 1 Neon Green Sheet (layered stickers)
  - 1 Zig-Zag Zebra™ Sheet (bag cover)
  - 1 Denim Roll (bag cover)
  - 1 Skulls Roll (bag cover)
  - 1 Gold Roll (bag cover and bow)
  - 1 Mustache Roll (bag cover and rosette)
  - 1 Neon Yellow Roll (rosette)
- ❑ 1 Sealable Plastic Bag
- ❑ 1 Gemstone (rosette)
- ❑ Hook-and-Loop Fastener Circles with Adhesive Backing
- ❑ Nonstick Scissors
- ❑ Paper Trimmer (optional)
- ❑ Cork-Backed Ruler
- ❑ Cutting Mat (optional)

ATTACH THE REMAINING STRIPS. Continue adding strips of tape to the bag at an angle, making sure each new strip slightly overlaps the previous one. Add strips until only a small portion of the bag remains uncovered.

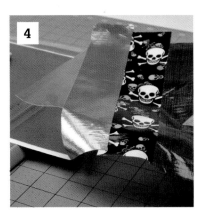

CUT THE LAST PIECE. When only a small portion of the bag is left uncovered, lay the uncovered area over a sheet of duct tape and use it as a guide to cut a piece from the sheet that matches the uncovered area.

ATTACH THE LAST PIECE. Attach the last piece of tape to the bag.

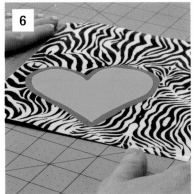

COVER THE OTHER SIDE. Decorate the other side of the bag using the same method you did before, or cover it with a single sheet of duct tape and add sticker embellishments.

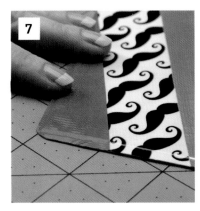

SEAL AND TRIM. Once both sides of the bag are covered, run your thumbnail along the edge of the bag to create a tight seal. Trim the excess tape from the edges of the bag, creating an even border. If desired, round the bottom corners for extra flair.

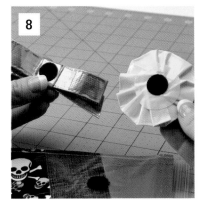

EMBELLISH. Embellish the bag by creating bows or rosettes. Then, attach them to the bag using circular hook-and-loop fasteners. Attach the loop pieces to the bag and the hook pieces to the embellishments.

ADHESIVE ADVICE

Reuse your duct tape sandwich bags by turning them inside out and carefully washing the insides with warm, soapy water.

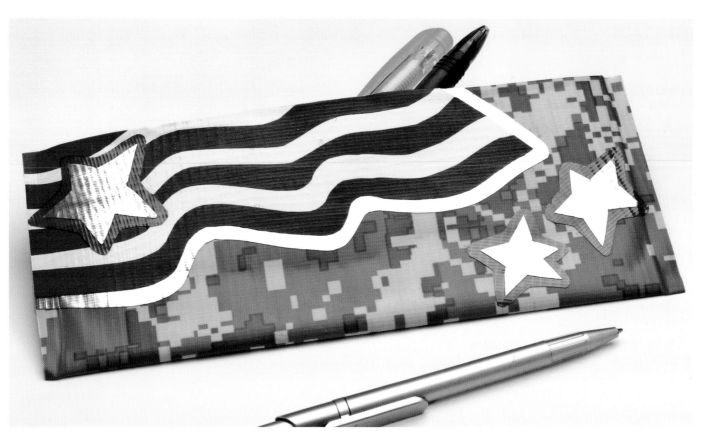

Pencil Case

A customized pencil case is a great way to show off your style and personality. Create a girly look with bright colors and lots of embellishments, or go for a rebellious punk rock vibe with flame and skull duct tape patterns. You can even make a patriotic-themed pencil case like the one I created. This project can also be scaled up to make a satchel for carrying important papers or items. You can even adapt the design to create a secure duct tape wallet for your lunch money.

Tools and Materials

- ❑ Duct Tape:
  - • 1 Digital Camo Sheet (pencil case, outside)
  - • 1 Totally Tie-Dye™ Sheet (pencil case, liner)
  - • 1 Red Sheet (flag)
  - • 1 White Sheet (flag and stars)
  - • 1 Chrome Sheet (flag)
  - • 1 Blue Roll (stars)
- ❑ Hook-and-Loop Fastener Strips with Adhesive Backing
- ❑ Nonstick Scissors
- ❑ Paper Trimmer (optional)
- ❑ Cork-Backed Ruler
- ❑ Cutting Mat (optional)

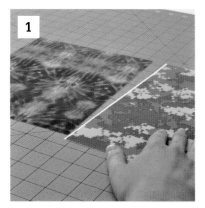

1

SELECT THE MATERIALS AND TRIM. Select two full-size sheets of duct tape, one for the liner of your pencil case and one for the outside. Trim the liner sheet to a smaller size by cutting away the first row of squares on all four sides of the sheet. Remember: You can save the strips for a future project.

85

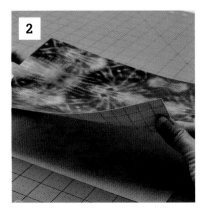

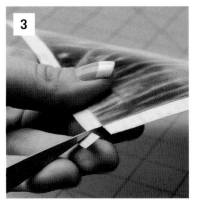

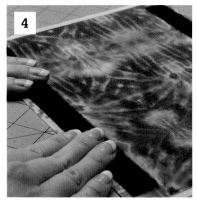

ATTACH THE SHEETS. Remove the paper backing from the outside pencil case sheet and place it sticky side up on your work surface. With the paper backing still attached, adhere the liner sheet, pattern side up, to the center of the outside pencil case sheet.

NOTCH THE CORNERS AND FOLD OVER THE EDGES. Cut square notches from all four corners of the outside sheet. Then, fold the edges of the outside sheet over the liner sheet along the two opposing long sides.

ATTACH THE FASTENERS. With the liner side of the pencil case still facing up, attach corresponding hook-and-loop fastener strips to each of the long edges of the pencil case. Place the fasteners about ³⁄₁₆" (5mm) below the edge of the sheet and about ¼" (6mm) away from each end.

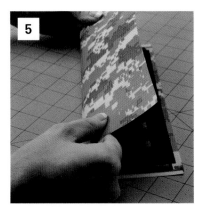

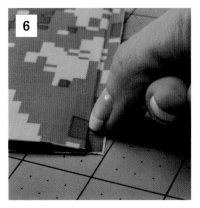

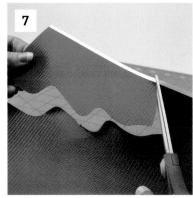

FOLD THE CASE. Fold the pencil case in half lengthwise, so the hook-and-loop fasteners join. Crease the bottom of the case.

SEAL THE CASE. Run your thumbnail along both sides of the pencil case to create a good seal, and trim away any exposed sticky portions of tape.

CUT THE FLAG SHAPE. To make the flag, cut a piece from the corner of a sheet of red duct tape, cutting a wavy pattern along the bottom edge. Cutting from the corner of the sheet will ensure the edges along the top and side of the flag are perpendicular.

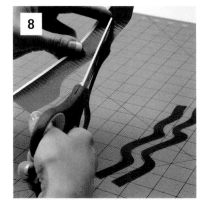

CUT THE RED STRIPES. Cut the red sheet from the previous step into four parallel ½" (13mm)-wide strips, following the wavy pattern you cut at the bottom of the piece.

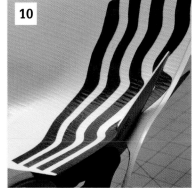

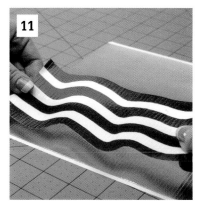

ATTACH THE RED STRIPES. Remove the paper backing from the red strips and attach them in an evenly spaced manner to the corner of a white sheet of duct tape.

CUT OUT THE FLAG. Cut the flag from the white sheet by trimming along the bottom edge of the lowest red strip, up the right side, across the top of the highest red strip, and down the left side.

ATTACH THE FLAG. Remove the paper backing from the flag and place it on the corner of a chrome sheet of tape, about ½" (13mm) from the bottom edge.

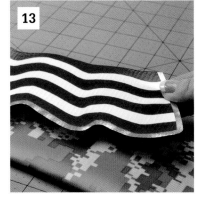

CUT THE BORDER. Trim around the flag, leaving a ³⁄₁₆" (5mm)-wide border around each edge.

ATTACH THE FLAG. Remove the paper backing from the flag and attach it to the pencil case, aligning the left edge of the flag with the left edge of the case. Position the flag so it completely covers the upper left corner of the case (some of it will extend over the edges).

TRIM AND EMBELLISH. Once your flag is in place, trim away any portions that extend past the edges of the case. Embellish the case with layered duct tape stickers (see page 20) and other decorative elements as desired.

ADHESIVE ADVICE

When creating layered duct tape stickers, use metallic duct tape for the bottom-most layer to make the shapes really pop.

Pocket Protector

This geek-chic project is a duct tape twist on the classic 1960s pocket protector. With bright colors and plenty of bling, this piece is stylish, functional, studious, and definitely meant to stand out. Use it to add some professional panache to a traditional button-down shirt, or tuck it in the back pocket of your jeans for a convenient way to transport your pens from class to class. Complete the look with a small strip of duct tape around the bridge of your glasses.

POCKET PROTECTOR

MEASURE AND TRIM THE MATERIALS. The pocket protector is made from two liner sheets, two outside sheets, and two flap sheets. To determine the size of the sheets you need, measure your shirt pocket. Cut the two outside sheets so they are slightly smaller than the width of the pocket and 2"–3" (51–76mm) longer than the height of the pocket. Cut the two liner sheets so they are ½" (13mm) smaller in width and 2"–3" (51–76mm) smaller in height than the outside sheets. The flap sheets will be cut in a later step.

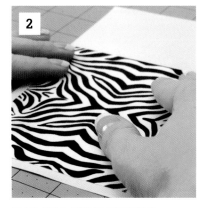

ATTACH A LINER SHEET. Remove the paper backing from one of the outside sheets and place it sticky side up. Remove the paper backing from one of the liner sheets and attach it, sticky side down, to the outside sheet. Place the liner sheet so it is about ¼" (6mm) from the bottom and each side of the outside sheet.

CUT AND ATTACH A FLAP SHEET. Measure the distance from the top of the liner sheet to the top of the outside sheet. Cut the two flap pieces that are this height and the width of the outside sheet. Remove the paper backing from one of the flap pieces and adhere it, color side up, to the top of the outside sheet, aligning the bottom edge of the flap sheet with the top edge of the liner sheet. Trim away any portions of the flap sheet that extend past the sides of the outside sheet.

Tools and Materials

- ❑ Duct Tape:
  - • 2 (or more) Neon Pink Sheets depending on the size of your pocket (protector, outside and flaps)
  - • 2 Zig-Zag Zebra™ Sheets (protector, liner)
  - • 1 Zig-Zag Zebra™ Roll (ruffle and glasses tape)
  - • 1 Denim Roll (ruffle)
  - • 1 Chrome Sheet or Roll (flap accent)
- ❑ Gemstones (protector and glasses tape)
- ❑ Hook-and-Loop Fastener Circles with Adhesive Backing (glasses tape)
- ❑ Nonstick Scissors
- ❑ Paper Trimmer (optional)
- ❑ Cork-Backed Ruler
- ❑ Hot Glue Gun
- ❑ Glue Sticks
- ❑ Cutting Mat (optional)

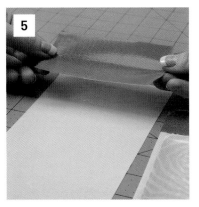

PLACE THE SECOND LINER SHEET. Remove the paper backing from the remaining liner sheet and place it, pattern side down on top of the first liner sheet, carefully aligning the edges.

ATTACH THE SECOND FLAP SHEET. Remove the paper backing from the remaining outside sheet and place it sticky side up on your work surface. Remove the paper backing from the remaining flap sheet and attach it, sticky side down, to the top of the second outside sheet.

CREATE THE POCKET. Attach the second outside sheet from the previous step to the pocket layers that have already been assembled. Carefully align the edges of the outside sheets as you attach them.

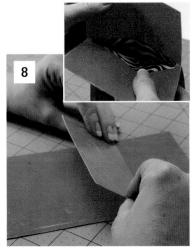

SEAL THE POCKET. Run your thumbnail along the edges of the liner sheets to create a good seal, and trim away any exposed sticky portions of tape. Trim around the edges of the pocket to create an even border.

FOLD THE FLAP. Fold down the front flap and crease it.

ADD RUFFLES. If desired, attach two layers of ruffles to the front flap. Align the bottom edge of the second ruffle with the bottom edge of the tape strip used to secure the first ruffle. This will help you keep your ruffles evenly spaced.

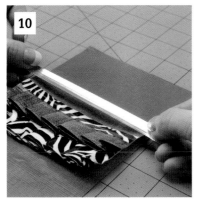

ADD ADDITIONAL TAPE STRIPS.
Attach a ⅜" (10mm)-wide strip
of tape to the flap to add some
extra flair.

EMBELLISH WITH GEMSTONES.
Hot glue gemstones to the upper
flap of the pocket protector as you
desire. Remember that you can
embellish your projects any way you
want using rosettes, stickers, strips of
tape, and other decorative items.

CUT THE TOP EDGE. Cut a wavy
edge along the top of the pocket
protector. If desired, round the
bottom corners.

GLASSES TAPE

FOLD A THIN STRIP. Cut a piece of
tape long enough to wrap around
the bridge of your glasses, with an
additional ½" (13mm) to allow for
overlap. Fold this piece into a thin
strip, using the method described on
page 14.

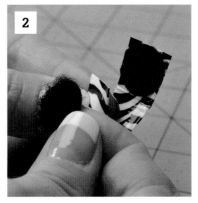

ATTACH THE FASTENERS. Attach
hook-and-loop fastener circles to
each end of the strip. Attach the
hook piece to the BACK side and the
loop piece to the FRONT side.

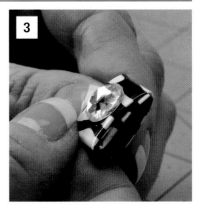

EMBELLISH. Add small gemstones
or stickers to the strip as desired.

Book Covers

School is for work and learning, but it's also for fun and friends. Recess and lunch are times to relax and enjoy a break from classes with your peers, and everyone knows one of the best ways to unwind is by playing games. Recess favorites like tag and hopscotch are lots of fun and great exercise, but not always practical during rainy days or in a lunchroom. In situations like this, indulge in a mental challenge instead of a physical one with a fun game of tic-tac-toe or checkers. These book covers are custom designed to act as your playing board, with an accompanying pocket to hold your game pieces. The pocket can also be used to hold a deck of playing cards, flashcards for studying, or supplies like pencils and erasers. If you're looking for something a little more decorative, you can use layered duct tape stickers and rosettes to design a book cover with interchangeable flowers.

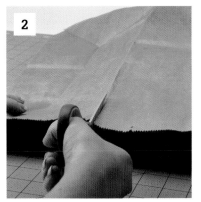

SELECT AND CUT THE BAG. Select a paper bag large enough to cover your book and cut away the bottom.

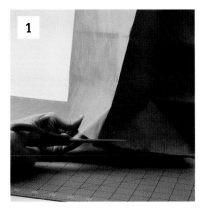

CUT THE SIDE. Cut along one of the side seams of the bag so you are left with a large sheet you can lay flat.

Tools and Materials

- ❑ Duct Tape:
  - • 4 (or more) Purple Sheets depending on the size of your book (book cover)
  - • 2–3 Zig-Zag Zebra™ Sheets (cover trim, playing grid, and pocket)
  - • 1 Skulls Roll (X pieces)
  - • 1 Pink Zebra Roll (O pieces)
- ❑ Gemstones (O pieces)
- ❑ Paper bag
- ❑ Hook-and-Loop Fastener Circles with Adhesive Backing
- ❑ Nonstick Scissors
- ❑ Cork-Backed Ruler
- ❑ Hot Glue Gun
- ❑ Glue Sticks
- ❑ Cutting Mat (optional)

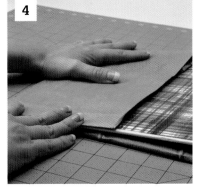

FOLD THE EDGES. Open your book and place it on top of the bag. Using the book as a guide, fold the top and bottom edge of the bag over so the height of the bag matches the height of the book. When you have folded the edges over, place the book on top of the bag.

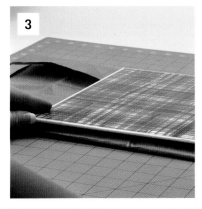

FOLD THE ENDS. Using the book as a guide, fold one end of the bag over the front cover of the book and crease it. Repeat with the back cover. Don't wrap the covers too tightly, or you won't be able to close the book.

ATTACH THE COVER. Tuck the front and back covers into the pockets you've created in the paper bag sheet.

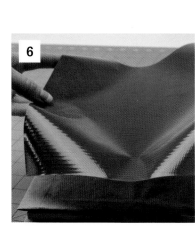

COVER THE BAG. Use duct tape sheets to completely cover the bag. Tape the front and back covers and along the spine.

WRAP THE CORNERS. Wrap the corners of the cover where the book has been tucked into the bag. Trim as needed to avoid getting tape directly on the book.

ADD TRIM. Create trim along the top and bottom of the book by attaching strips of tape along the edges. Place the trim strips across the front of the book, around the spine, and across the back.

CREATE A PLAYING BOARD. I used four thin strips of tape to create a tic-tac-toe playing board on the front cover of the book. You can make your book cover into a board for almost any game played on a grid, such as checkers, chess, or Parcheesi. You can even make a puzzle!

ATTACH THE FASTENERS. Place the loop pieces of circular hook-and-loop fasteners in the center of each square in your grid.

MAKE THE FIRST SET OF PLAYING PIECES. I made X pieces for my board by creating two folded thin strips of the same length, crossing them over one another, and securing them with an additional strip of tape. Make five X pieces for a tic-tac-toe board.

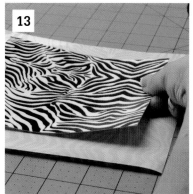

MAKE THE SECOND SET OF PLAYING PIECES AND ATTACH FASTENERS. Make five rosettes for the O pieces. Attach the hook pieces of circular hook-and-loop fasteners to the back of each playing piece.

CUT AND ATTACH THE POCKET SHEETS. To make a pocket for your book, cut a rectangular sheet of duct tape 1" (25mm) smaller on all sides than the inside portion of the book's cover. Then, trim a second piece that is 1" (25mm) smaller on all sides than the first piece. Remove the paper backing from the large sheet and place it sticky side up. Place the small sheet, pattern side up with the paper backing still on, in the center of the large sheet.

NOTCH TWO CORNERS. Cut square notches in two opposing corners of the large sheet.

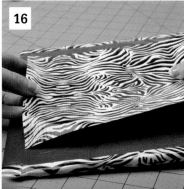

ADHESIVE ADVICE

If desired, add a flap with hook-and-loop fasteners to your pocket for extra security.

FOLD OVER THE EDGE. Fold the edge of tape with the notched corners over onto the small sheet.

ATTACH THE POCKET. Attach the pocket to the inside of the front cover, making sure the side of the sheet with the folded edge is at the top. Use the pocket to store your game pieces.

Insulated Lunch Bag

Covering items like lunch boxes with duct tape to give them a new appearance is a classic duct tape trick and a great way to quickly revamp an existing object. This project takes your skills to the next level, showing you how to create your own insulated lunch bag using only duct tape, bubble wrap, and hook-and-loop fasteners. As with every project, you can design your lunch bag to have a clean, simple look, or step it up by piling on the ruffles, rosettes, and stickers.

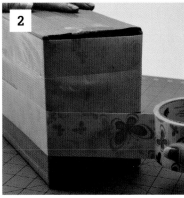

SELECT A BOX AND BEGIN WRAPPING. Select a cardboard box of the size you would like your lunch bag to be. Cover the bottom and side of the box with tape, leaving the top uncovered. To begin, unroll a length of tape and wrap it around the top edge of the box with the sticky side facing AWAY from the box. When you reach the starting end of the strip, trim the strip from the roll and secure it in place by overlapping the strip ends.

FINISH WRAPPING THE BOX. Continue wrapping the box in strips of tape, placing each row of tape so it slightly overlaps the previous one. Make sure the sticky side is FACING you. Wrap the final strip of tape around the bottom of the box so the tape extends slightly beyond the edge.

Tools and Materials

- ❑ Duct Tape:
  - • 5–6 Cosmic Tie-Dye™ Sheets depending on the desired size of your lunch bag (bag and lid, outside)
  - • 1 Butterfly Roll (bag and lid, liner)
  - • 1 Totally Tie-Dye™ Roll (handles and rosettes)
  - • 1 Peace Sign Roll (handles and rosettes)
  - • 1 Neon Yellow Roll (rosette)
  - • 1 Cosmic Tie-Dye™ Roll (seams and patching)
- ❑ Cardboard Box (lunch bag form)
- ❑ Bubble Wrap
- ❑ Clear Packaging Tape
- ❑ Cover Button Kit (rosette)
- ❑ 1 Gemstone (rosette)
- ❑ Hook-and-Loop Fastener Strips with Adhesive Backing
- ❑ Nonstick Scissors
- ❑ Cork-Backed Ruler
- ❑ Flexible Tape Measure
- ❑ Cutting Mat (optional)
- ❑ Hot Glue Gun
- ❑ Glue Sticks

FOLD THE CORNERS. On the bottom of the box, fold in the corners of the last row of tape like you are wrapping a present and fold the tape over the edges of the box.

COVER THE BOTTOM. Take strips of tape and place them, sticky side UP along the bottom of the box until it is covered. Fold any excess portions of tape over the sides of the box.

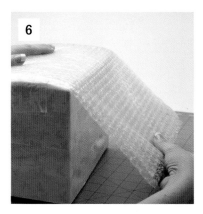

CUT THE BUBBLE WRAP TO SIZE.
Place two layers of bubble wrap on top of one another and cut them to a width that matches the width of the front of the box.

ATTACH THE BUBBLE WRAP.
Attach the bubble wrap to the front, bottom, and back of the box, trimming away any excess as needed.

SECURE THE BUBBLE WRAP. Use clear packaging tape to secure the edges of the bubble wrap along the top of the box as needed.

ADHESIVE ADVICE

When using the bubble wrap, place the two layers so the bubbles are facing each other, giving you a flat outer surface with which to work.

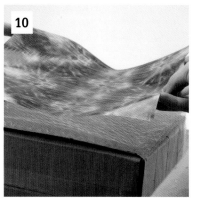

COVER THE SIDES WITH BUBBLE WRAP. Place two layers of bubble wrap on top of one another and cut them to the dimensions of one of the sides of the box. Using clear packaging tape, attach the bubble wrap layers to one of the box sides. Repeat to cover the remaining side of the box.

COVER ONE SIDE. Cut a sheet of duct tape to the appropriate size and use it to cover one of the sides of the box. Wrap any excess tape around the edges, folding the corners as needed as shown in step 3.

COVER THE REST OF THE BOX.
Cover the remaining side, front, and back of the box with duct tape sheets. Then, cut a sheet to the exact size of the bottom of the box and press it in place, using it to cover any edges of tape you folded over onto the bottom.

COVER THE EDGES. Remove the box from the lunch bag by pressing against the bottom with your thumbs while holding the lunch bag in place with your fingers. Cover the upper edges of the bag by measuring and cutting a strip of tape the length of the front of the bag and pressing it to the inner side of the front of the bag, allowing half of the tape to extend past the edge. Then, fold the excess tape down along the outside of the box. Repeat to cover the upper edges of the back and sides.

MEASURE AND CUT BUBBLE WRAP FOR THE LID. Place two layers of bubble wrap on top of one another. Align one edge of the bubble wrap assembly with the back edge of the lunch bag. Trim the edges of the bubble wrap so it extends 1½" (38mm) beyond the edges of the front and sides of the bag.

MEASURE AND CUT TAPE FOR THE LID. Measure and cut a sheet of duct tape that is about 1" (25mm) larger on all sides than the bubble wrap you cut for the lid during the previous step. If necessary, patch duct tape sheets together as shown.

ATTACH THE BUBBLE WRAP. Place the lid sheet sticky side up and attach the bubble wrap for the lid, centering it in the sheet of tape.

NOTCH THE CORNERS. Cut square notches from all four corners of the sheet.

FOLD OVER THE EDGES. Fold the edges of the tape over the bubble wrap on all four sides.

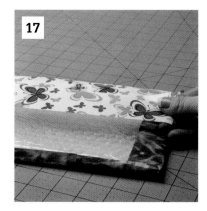

LINE THE LID. Cover the bottom of the lid with strips of tape that coordinate with the interior pattern of your lunch bag.

ATTACH THE LID. Lay the lunch bag on its back, and align the top edge of the lunch bag with the corresponding edge of the lid. Connect the lid to the bag with a strip of tape.

SECURE THE LID. Set the lunch bag upright and close the lid. Attach a strip of tape to the outer seam between the lid and the bag.

TRIM A CORNER. Close the lid and pinch one of the front corners together. Then, trim the excess from the corner.

TAPE THE CORNER. Holding the edges of the trimmed corner together, place a strip of tape around the corner to secure it in place. Trim and tape the other corner. Patch the corners on the inside of the lid as needed.

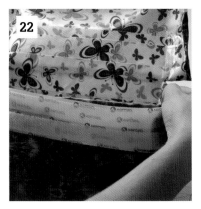

ATTACH FASTENERS TO THE BAG. Using the bag as a guide, measure and trim hook-and-loop fastener strips long enough to wrap around the top edge of the front and two sides of the lunch bag. Attach the hook piece to the top edge of the bag and the loop piece to the inside edge of the lid.

MEASURE AND CUT THE HANDLES. The ends of the lunch bag handles will be attached to the bottom of the bag and extend up the sides. With this in mind, determine the length of your handles. Measure and cut a strip of tape of this length from a roll, placing it sticky side up. Cut shorter strips of tape and attach them, sticky side down, to the handle strip, working from the center out toward the ends. Leave portions of the handle strip uncovered at each end. The amount of uncovered tape should match the distance from the center of the bottom of the bag to about 3" (76mm) from the top edge of the front of the bag.

ATTACH ONE END. Position one end of the handle strip over the front of the bag, placing it so the sticky portion of the strip is about 3" (76mm) below the top edge of the bag. Attach the strip to the side and bottom of the bag.

ATTACH THE OTHER END. Repeat this process with the other end of the handle, again positioning the sticky portion of tape so it is about 3" (76mm) from the top edge of the bag.

REINFORCE THE HANDLE. Fold the handle down and make sure the ends are even. Reinforce the handle by placing small strips of tape over the handle strap where it connects to the lunch bag.

PATCH THE HANDLES. Hide the strips of tape used to reinforce the handles with pieces of tape that match the color or pattern of tape you used for the outside of the lunch bag. Repeat steps 23 through 27 to make and attach the second handle. Embellish the bag with rosettes or other decorative items as desired.

CHAPTER 3:
Duct Tape Décor

You've added duct tape crafts to your wardrobe, shown them off at school, and now it's time to duct tape your digs. These projects are a great way to bring trendy functionality to any room, or to add a splash of color to your car or doorway. One of the best reasons to use duct tape for room décor is—it's easy to change! If you create a chandelier with black and flame duct tape and, a month later, decide you want a neon pink one instead, you can switch it up in a jiffy. Altering duct tape projects is much simpler, faster, and cheaper than painting your walls or buying a new comforter, blanket, and sheets.

Duct tape projects like these are also great for dorm rooms or college apartments because they are full of personality. You can also repair them easily if they get caught in the crossfire during a water balloon or silly string fight. Plus, what better way to meet new people than by showing off all you can do with just a few rolls of duct tape?

Wall-Mounted Storage Pocket

This handy duct tape pocket can be mounted on any wall or door you desire and can be removed easily to travel with you when you leave. You can also put hangers for it in your locker so it can move between home and school. Place your finished homework in it each night and take it to school with you the next day to be stored in your locker. Use it to hold important letters, store memories like photos and concert tickets, or keep items you use every day, like your hairbrush.

SELECT THE MATERIALS AND TRIM. Select two full-size sheets of duct tape of the same color or pattern for the outside of the pocket and two for the pocket liner. Reduce the size of the liner sheets by trimming away the first row of squares from all four sides.

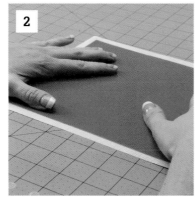

ATTACH A LINER SHEET. Remove the paper backing from one of the outside sheets and place it sticky side up. Attach one of the liner sheets, color side up with the paper backing still on, centering it in the outside sheet.

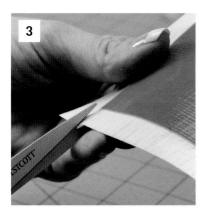

CUT TWO NOTCHES. At the opposing corners on either end of one of the long sides of the sheet, cut a line from the edge of the outside sheet in to the corner of the liner sheet.

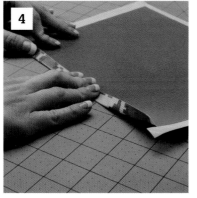

FOLD OVER THE EDGE. Fold the notched edge of the outside sheet over the liner sheet.

MAKE AND ATTACH THE SECOND SIDE. Repeat steps 2 through 4 to create the other side of the pocket. Then, attach the two sides, making sure the edges are aligned.

WARNING

Duct tape projects are great for decorating concrete or cement dorm room walls, but do not apply duct tape directly to painted surfaces, or you risk damaging the paint when you remove the project. Use duct tape projects to decorate dorm room furniture, storage containers, lampshades, and other unpainted surfaces!

Tools and Materials

- ❑ Duct Tape:
  - • 2 Digital Camo Sheets (pocket, outside)
  - • 2 Neon Pink Sheets (pocket, liner)
  - • 1 Digital Camo Roll (rosette and embellishment strips)
  - • 1 Neon Yellow Roll (rosette and embellishment strips)
- ❑ 1 Gemstone (rosette)
- ❑ 4 Plastic Curtain Grommets
- ❑ Marker
- ❑ Nonstick Scissors
- ❑ Paper Trimmer (optional)
- ❑ Cork-Backed Ruler
- ❑ Hot Glue Gun
- ❑ Glue Sticks
- ❑ Cutting Mat (optional)

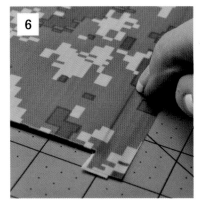

SEAL THE POCKET. Run your thumbnail along the edges of the pocket to create a tight seal.

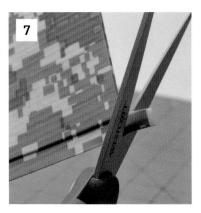

TRIM THE EDGES. Trim around the sides and bottom of the pocket to create an even border. Trim away the tabs at the top corners of the pocket. Round the bottom corners of the pocket if desired.

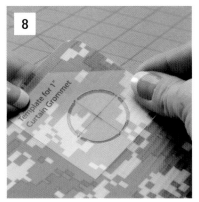

TRACE THE GROMMET TEMPLATE. Place a grommet template in one of the corners of the pocket. Trace the template. Measure the distance from the top and side of the pocket to the circle you drew for the grommet. Use the measurement to mark circles for the grommets in the remaining three corners of the pocket.

CUT A GROMMET HOLE AND PLACE A GROMMET. Cut out one of the grommet holes. Place the grommet bottom inside the pocket and push it up through the hole. Position the grommet top over the grommet bottom and snap it in place.

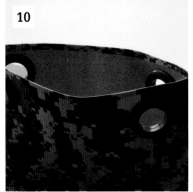

PLACE THE REMAINING GROMMETS. Cut out the remaining three grommet holes and place the remaining grommets.

EMBELLISH. Add embellishments to the pocket as desired. I added a layered rosette with four folded thin strips that I trimmed at an angle.

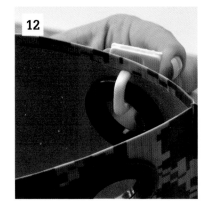

MOUNT THE POCKET. Select adhesive hooks that fit the grommets and use them to mount the pocket on a wall or door. You could also use suction cups with hooks to mount the pocket to a smooth surface.

Vase

You might find it hard to believe at first, but this is not a purely decorative item. It's a fully functional vase you can use to house beautiful bouquets from your garden or your special someone. You can mount it on your wall using hooks, like with the Wall-Mounted Storage Pocket (page 104), or you can mount it on glass using suction cups, giving you the option to brighten up your windows or mirrors with some natural blooms. While the instructions explain how to make a simple geometrically shaped vase (above right), the technique can be used to create a vase in a variety of cool shapes (above left).

Tools and Materials

- ❑ Duct Tape:
  - • 2 Cosmic Tie-Dye™ Sheets (vase, outside)
  - • 2 Neon Yellow Sheets (vase, liner)
- ❑ Gemstones (vase embellishments)
- ❑ 1 Plastic Curtain Grommet
- ❑ Marker
- ❑ Wall Hook or Suction Cup
- ❑ Nonstick Scissors
- ❑ Paper Trimmer (optional)
- ❑ Cork-Backed Ruler
- ❑ Hot Glue Gun
- ❑ Glue Sticks
- ❑ Cutting Mat (optional)

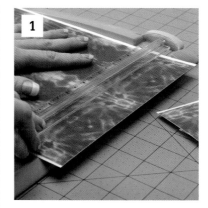

SELECT THE MATERIALS AND TRIM. Select two sheets of duct tape of the same color or pattern for the vase liner and trim them so they are 7¼" (184mm) square. Select two additional sheets of duct tape of the same color or pattern for the outside of the vase and trim them so they are 8¼" (210mm) square.

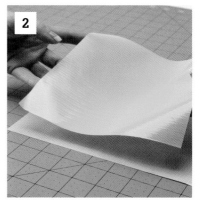

ATTACH A LINER SHEET. Remove the paper backing from one of the outside sheets and place it sticky side up. Then, remove the paper backing from one of the liner sheets and attach it, sticky side down, to the outside sheet. Make sure you center the liner sheet in the outside sheet.

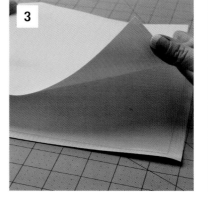

ADD THE SECOND LINER SHEET. Remove the paper backing from the remaining liner sheet and place it, color side down, directly on top of the first liner sheet, making sure the edges and corners are aligned.

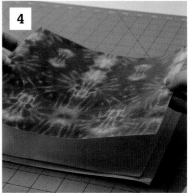

ATTACH THE REMAINING OUTSIDE SHEET. Remove the paper backing from the remaining outside sheet and place it, sticky side down, on top of the other vase layers already assembled. Make sure you align the edges and corners of the two outside sheets.

SEAL THE VASE. Run your thumbnail along the edges of the vase to ensure a tight seal.

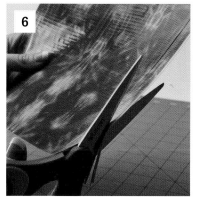

TRIM. Trim around the edges of the vase to create an even border. Make sure you don't cut into the center liner pieces while trimming.

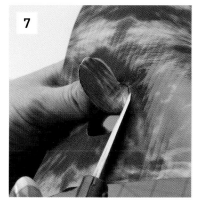

CUT A GROMMET HOLE. Place a grommet template in one of the vase corners and trace it. Then, cut out the grommet hole, cutting through all four layers of tape. When you are finished, you should be able to see straight through the hole in the corner of the vase.

ATTACH THE GROMMET. Place the grommet bottom beneath the vase, positioning it under the grommet hole. Snap the grommet top in place, making sure you capture all four layers of duct tape in the grommet.

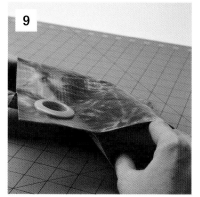

CUT THE EDGES. Cut open the edges of the vase on each side of the grommet by aligning your scissors with the edge of the liner sheets and cutting away the border.

EMBELLISH. Embellish the vase with gemstones, or decorate it using another method of your choice.

Rearview Mirror Dice

Passing your driver's test is a huge rite of passage, and borrowing the keys to the family car for a night is perhaps an even bigger one. But what trumps them all is getting a car you can call your very own, whether it's a shiny new model or an indestructible hand-me-down. The best part of having your own car is you can decorate it any way you want. You can show off your school spirit with a window sticker, display your interests or favorite vacation destinations on bumper stickers, and wrap your steering wheel in fuzzy leopard-print cloth. You can also make your very own set of duct tape dice to hang from your rearview mirror. Of course these larger-than-life game pieces aren't limited to your car. Hang them in your school locker or from the ceiling of your room. If you do intend to use them for your car, please review your state and local laws regarding driving safety. Some states and counties prohibit hanging objects from your rearview mirror because of safety concerns.

MEASURE, CUT, AND FOLD THE HANGER. Measure and trim a 22" (559mm)-long piece of tape from a roll. Make it into a folded thin strip using the method described on page 14.

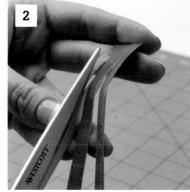

CREATE A FRINGE. Cut the folded strip lengthwise into three equally sized pieces. Stop cutting about ½" (13mm) from the top of the strip so the three pieces remain connected.

Tools and Materials

- ❏ Duct Tape:
  - • 1–2 Neon Pink Sheets (dice sides)
  - • 1 Spotted Leopard Sheet (dice sides)
  - • 1 Checker Roll (dice sides)
  - • 1 Neon Pink Roll (dice hanger)
- ❏ 2 Polystyrene Foam (Styrofoam™) Cubes (3" [76mm] square)
- ❏ Gemstones (number dots)
- ❏ Clear Packaging Tape (if needed)
- ❏ Nonstick Scissors
- ❏ Cork-Backed Ruler
- ❏ Hot Glue Gun
- ❏ Glue Sticks
- ❏ Cutting Mat (optional)

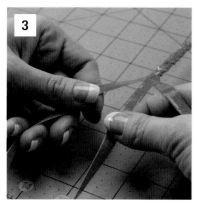

BRAID THE STRIP. Secure the end of the strip to your work surface with a small scrap piece of tape. Then, braid the three sections of the strip together.

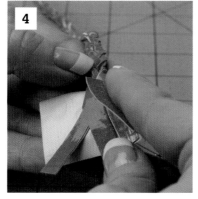

SECURE THE BRAID. With a small piece of scrap tape, secure the end of the braid. Pull gently on both ends of the braid to stretch it.

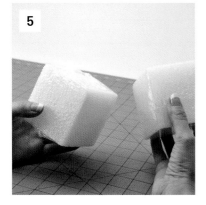

5

6

7

SELECT THE DICE CUBES. Select two 3" (76mm)-square polystyrene foam cubes still wrapped in their plastic packaging. If your cubes are unwrapped, cover them in clear packaging tape. The plastic packaging (or packaging tape) provides a better sticking surface for the duct tape than the foam itself.

ATTACH THE BRAID. Use 3" (76mm)-long pieces of tape to attach each end of the braid to a top corner of each of the cubes.

SECURE THE BRAID. Use additional pieces of tape to secure the underside of each end of the braid.

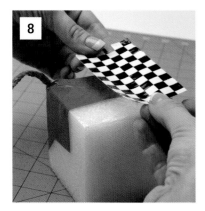

8

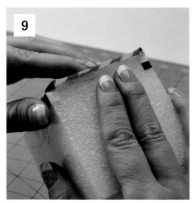

9

10

BEGIN COVERING THE CUBE. Take a strip of tape and attach it to the top of a cube (the side with the braid attached). Allow the tape to extend slightly past the edges of the cube, wrapping the excess down over the sides.

FOLD IN THE CORNERS. Fold the corners of the tape in as if you were wrapping a present, and fold the excess tape down over the edge of the cube.

FINISH COVERING THE TOP. Cover the remaining exposed area on the top of the cube with another strip of tape. Cut a notch in the tape, near the braid. If desired, you can use sheets of duct tape cut to size to cover the sides of the cube.

COVER THE BRAID. Wrap the notched piece of tape cut during the previous step around the braid and secure it to the side of the cube.

COVER THE BOTTOM. Use strips to cover the opposite side of the cube, wrapping the excess tape around the edges as before.

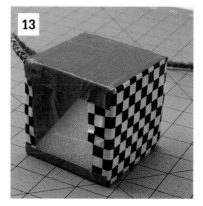

COVER TWO OPPOSING SIDES. Cover two opposing sides of the cube with tape. You can wrap excess tape over the edges of the cube that have not yet been decorated, but don't wrap tape over the top and bottom sides of the cube. Trim away any excess if necessary.

COVER THE REMAINING SIDES. For the remaining uncovered sides of the cube, cut two 3" (76mm)-square pieces of tape from a sheet. These squares will be used to cover any rough edges created by wrapping tape around the sides of the cube during the previous steps. Remove the paper backing from the squares and place them on the undecorated sides of the cube, carefully aligning the edges of the tape with the edges of the cube.

MARK THE NUMBER DOTS. Mark the number dots on the sides of the die by denting the foam using your scissors.

ATTACH THE NUMBER DOTS. Glue gems or place stickers over the dents you made during the previous step to create the number dots on the sides of the die. If desired, you could also cut numbers from duct tape and place these on the appropriate sides. Decorate the other die and hang the pair from your rearview mirror or in your room as a decoration.

Tools and Materials

- ❑ Duct Tape:
  - • 1 Neon Pink Roll (rosettes)
  - • 1 Peace Sign Roll (rosettes)
  - • 1 Polka Dot Roll (rosettes)
  - • 1 Zig-Zag Roll (rosettes)
- ❑ 1 Gallon-Sized Plastic Water or Juice Bottle
- ❑ 4-Watt Nightlight and Fixture
- ❑ Cover Button Kit (rosettes)
- ❑ Nonstick Scissors
- ❑ Hobby Knife
- ❑ Cutting Mat
- ❑ Cork-Backed Ruler
- ❑ Hot Glue Gun
- ❑ Glue Sticks

Water Bottle Chandelier

Repurposing an empty plastic bottle, this thrifty project is another great example of upcycling. Place this nightlight on a bedside table, or hang it from your ceiling to cast a colorful glow around your room. The shape of your plastic bottle will determine the design for this piece, so try to select one with an eye-catching, unique appearance. If you want to use this project in your bedroom, decorate it with colors that match your wallpaper, comforter, or sheets. You can even show off your school spirit by decorating it with your school colors or those of your favorite sports team.

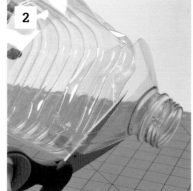

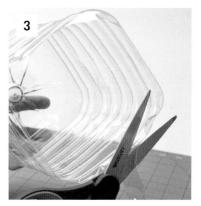

SELECT AND CUT THE PLASTIC BOTTLE. Select a plastic gallon-sized water or juice bottle of the shape you desire. Using a hobby knife, cut a circle from the bottom of the bottle large enough for the fixture of a 4-watt nightlight bulb to pass through. Keep your fingers clear of the knife as you cut. Young crafters: Have an adult help with this step.

REMOVE THE BOTTLE TOP. Make an incision at the top of the shoulder of your water bottle with your hobby knife. Then, insert the top blade of your scissors into the incision and cut away the top of the bottle.

EVEN OUT THE TOP EDGE. Trim around the top of the opening you cut to create a smooth, flat edge.

ADHESIVE ADVICE

To easily cut around the bottle's perimeter in a straight line, hold the bottle horizontally (on its side), and begin the cut by inserting the top blade of your scissors into the incision you made in the bottle.

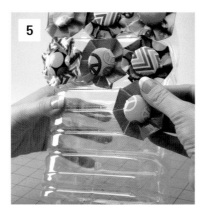

MAKE DECORATIVE ROSETTES. Make enough rosettes to cover your bottle. Use tape of different colors and patterns for the rosettes, and glue on gemstones, covered buttons, or other accent pieces as desired.

ATTACH THE ROSETTES. Hot glue the rosettes to the bottle, covering the entire surface. You could also decorate the bottle with strips of tape, rows of ruffles, or stickers.

INSERT THE LIGHT BULB. Insert the light fixture through the hole in the top of the chandelier. Place the light on a bedside table or hang it from your ceiling. Warning: DO NOT use a light bulb that produces more than 4 watts, or you risk melting the bottle's plastic and causing a fire.

ADHESIVE ADVICE

Lay the rosettes out on your worktable so you can arrange them to create different patterns before gluing them in place.

3-D Shapes & Strips Curtain

Beaded curtains are tons of fun, but this unique duct tape curtain is even groovier. You'll use the same method employed in the Keychain project (page 47) to make the shapes for your curtain. The shapes can be simple and geometric, or wild and crazy, all depending on your design aesthetic. Make it your own! Hang these strips in your doorway, or use them as a window dressing.

CREATE A SHAPE. The shapes for the curtain are created using the same method employed for the Keychain project (page 47). Cut a shape of the desired size from a sheet of duct tape. Then, cut a matching shape that is ½" (13mm) larger on all sides than the original shape.

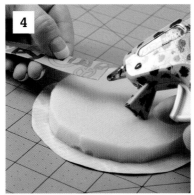

TRACE THE SMALL SHAPE. Trace the outline of the small shape on a piece of ½" (13mm) polyurethane foam and cut the shape from the foam.

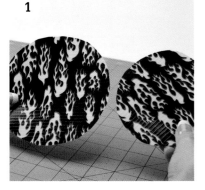

ATTACH THE FOAM SHAPE. Remove the paper backing from the large shape and place it on your work surface sticky side up. Center the foam piece on the large shape and attach it.

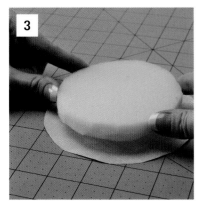

CREATE AND ATTACH TWO STRIPS. Measure and trim an 8" (203mm)-long strip of tape from a roll and make it into a folded thin strip using the method described on page 14. With the back of the strip facing up, glue 1½" (38mm) inches of one end of the strip to the foam. Create a second 8" (203mm)-long folded thin strip and glue it to the foam opposite the first strip.

Tools and Materials

- ❑ Duct Tape:
  - • 9 Flames Sheets (9 shapes)
  - • 9 Zig-Zag Zebra™ Sheets (9 shapes)
  - • 9 Electric Blue Sheets (9 shapes)
  - • 8 Spotted Leopard Sheets (8 shapes)
  - • 7 Neon Pink Sheets (7 shapes)
  - • 7 Purple Sheets (7 shapes)
  - • 1 Peace Sign Roll (1 strip)
  - • 1 Skulls Roll (1 strip)
  - • 1 Checker Roll (1 strip)
  - • 1 Paint Splatter Roll (2 strips)
  - • 1 Blue Plaid Roll (1 strip)
- ❑ Polyurethane Foam (½" [13mm] thick)
- ❑ Curtain Rod
- ❑ Nonstick Scissors
- ❑ Hobby Knife
- ❑ Cutting Mat
- ❑ Cork-Backed Ruler
- ❑ Hot Glue Gun
- ❑ Glue Sticks

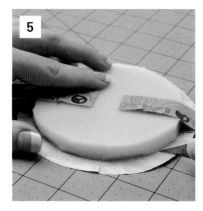

NOTCH THE TAPE. Cut notches ½" (13mm) apart in the exposed duct tape of the large shape.

PLACE THE SMALL SHAPE. Place the small shape, with the paper backing still attached, pattern side up on top of the foam piece.

FOLD OVER THE EDGES. Fold the notched pieces of tape you cut previously over the top of the small shape to secure it. Press the foam down as you work to ensure no gaps form. Do this for all the pieces except the ones located below the attached folded thin strips.

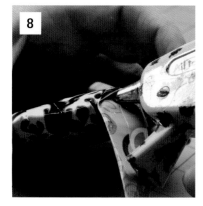

GLUE THE GAPS. Put a dab of hot glue in the gaps between the edge of the small shape and the back of each strip to close them.

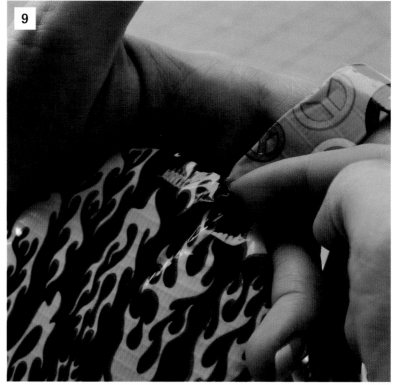

FOLD OVER THE REMAINING NOTCHED PIECES. Trim the remaining notched pieces located below the attached strips. Fold the edges of the notched pieces over and tuck them down against the strips, pushing them into the shape. Close any remaining gaps with a dab of hot glue.

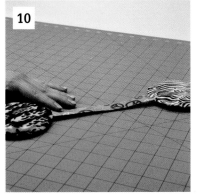

MAKE AND ATTACH A SECOND SHAPE. Make another shape and attach it to the end of one of the strips from the previous shape. Glue another strip to the opposite side of the new shape.

FINISH A FULL STRIP. Measure the window or doorway where you would like to place your curtain to determine the length of your curtain strips. Continue adding shapes and folded thin strips to your curtain strip until it is the length of your window or doorway.

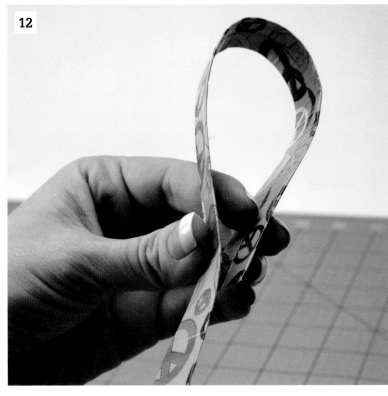

FINISH THE SHAPE STRIPS AND CREATE LOOPS. Create as many additional shape strips as you desire to cover your window or doorway. When you have the number you desire, make a loop large enough to fit over a curtain rod at the top end of each shape strip.

SECURE THE LOOP. Secure the loop at the top of each strip with a small piece of tape. Place the strips on a curtain rod and mount it over your window or doorway. If desired, wrap the curtain rod in duct tape.

Topiaries

A topiary is a tree or shrub that has been pruned or trimmed into a decorative shape. These duct tape topiaries are certainly not shrubbery, but they are reminiscent of some popular topiary forms. And while you can't color your backyard trees metallic and neon shades, you can make these plant-inspired creations any shape, color, or pattern you want. Duct tape topiaries make unique gifts and can vary in size depending on the size of the foam base you select. As always, cover them in embellishments like ruffles and rosettes for an extra-fun look.

TOPIARY³

SELECT THE BOTTOM CUBE AND COVER THE TOP. Select a 4½" x 5" (114 x 127mm) polystyrene foam cube with the plastic packaging still on it. If the cube is unwrapped, cover it with clear packaging tape. Cover the top of the cube with a sheet of duct tape, folding any excess over the edges and tucking in the corners like you are wrapping a present.

COVER THE BOTTOM. Flip the cube over and cover the bottom with a sheet of duct tape, wrapping the excess around the edges as before. You want the excess tape to extend about ½" (13mm) down all sides of the cube.

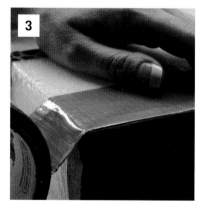

COVER THE TOP EDGE. Apply a strip of tape from a roll, aligning the top edge of the tape with the top edge of the cube.

FINISH COVERING THE EDGE. Continue applying tape, pressing it in place against the top edge of the cube, rotating the cube until the top edge of all four sides is covered.

Tools and Materials

- ❑ Duct Tape:

  - • 1 Green Sheet (bottom cube, top side)

  - • 1 Spotted Leopard Sheet (bottom cube, bottom side)

  - • 2–3 White Sheets (top cube)

  - • 1 Gold Roll (bottom cube sides, ruffle, large rosette, and small rosettes)

  - • 1 Pink Polka Dot Roll (ruffle and small rosettes)

  - • 1 Spotted Leopard Roll (bottom cube accent, large rosette, small rosettes, and dowel wrap)

  - • 1 Green Roll (large rosette)

- ❑ 2 Polystyrene Foam (Styrofoam™) Cubes (4½" x 5" [114 x 127mm])

- ❑ 1 Wooden Dowel (½" [13mm] diameter, 14" [356mm] long)

- ❑ Drill

- ❑ ½" (13mm) Drill Bit

- ❑ Cover Button Kit (small rosettes)

- ❑ Clear Packaging Tape (as needed)

- ❑ Nonstick Scissors

- ❑ Cork-Backed Ruler

- ❑ Hot Glue Gun

- ❑ Glue Sticks

- ❑ Cutting Mat (optional)

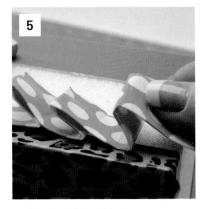

ATTACH A RUFFLE. Create a ruffle along the bottom edge of the sides of the cube, leaving a portion of the Spotted Leopard tape exposed. Apply the ruffle the whole way around the cube, patching it as needed.

SECURE THE RUFFLE. Tear a piece of tape from a roll and then tear it lengthwise to remove a thin strip. Use the thin strip to secure the edge of the ruffle.

ADD A SECOND RUFFLE. Attach a second ruffle, layering it over the first, and applying it the whole way around the cube. Align the bottom edge of the second ruffle with the bottom edge of the strip of tape you used to secure the first ruffle. Secure the second ruffle with a strip of tape.

ATTACH A FINAL RUFFLE. Add a third ruffle and secure it with a strip of tape as shown in the previous steps.

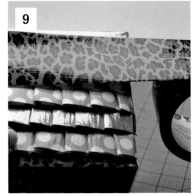

ADD A LAYER OF TAPE. Unroll a portion of tape and position it about ⅜" (10mm) from the top edge of the cube on one side. Press the tape in place. Continue applying the tape, pressing it in place until all four sides of the cube are wrapped.

ATTACH A ROSETTE AND DRILL. Create a three-layer rosette using the method employed for the Layered Rosette Bracelet project (page 37), minus the accent piece. Apply the rosette to the center of the top of the covered cube. Next, drill a ½" (13mm)-diameter hole about 4" (102mm) deep through the center of the rosette into the cube. Young crafters: Have an adult help with this step.

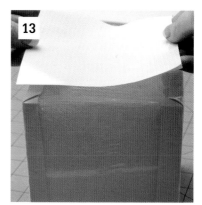

WRAP THE WOODEN DOWEL.
Measure and trim a 14" (356mm)-long strip of tape from a roll and use it to wrap your wooden dowel.

INSERT THE WOODEN DOWEL.
Insert the wooden dowel into the hole you drilled in the bottom cube of your topiary. If the fit is too tight, expand the hole slightly. Note: You want the wooden dowel to be secure enough to support the upper part of the topiary.

COVER AND DRILL THE UPPER CUBE. Take a second 4½" x 5" (114 x 127mm) polystyrene foam cube (wrapped in its plastic packaging or covered with clear packaging tape) and cover all the sides with tape. You can use sheets of tape to do this or strips from a roll. Drill a ½" (13mm)-diameter hole 4" (102mm) into the center of the bottom of the cube. Young crafters: Have an adult help with this step.

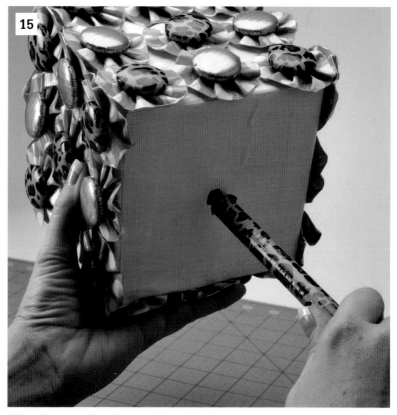

ADD ROSETTES. Cover the top and sides of the white cube with rosettes as desired, leaving the bottom of the cube (the side with the drilled hole) plain.

ATTACH THE TOP CUBE. Insert the other end of the covered wooden dowel into the hole of the rosette-covered cube.

TOPIARY VARIATIONS

LOLLIPOP TOPIARY

CREATE THE PETAL POINTS. Create multiple petal points for this topiary using the process you employed in the Petal Bracelet project (see page 32). Place the petal points in rows on your work surface for easy access.

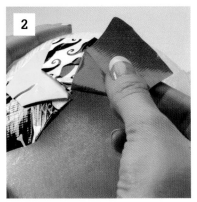

ATTACH THE PETAL POINTS. Apply the petal points to the bottom of a polystyrene foam sphere (in its original plastic packaging or wrapped in clear packaging tape), working in a circular pattern around a central point.

CLOSE THE RING. When you are ready to apply the last petal point in the circle, pick up the edge of the first petal point and tuck the end of the last one underneath it to create a continuous ring.

CONTINUE ADDING PETAL POINTS. Layer additional rings of petal points over the first ring and around the sphere until you reach the top.

COVER THE TOP OF THE SPHERE. Create a final ring of petal points at the top of the sphere. Then, cut several triangular pieces of duct tape and use them to cover any exposed areas at the center of the top ring. Drill a hole of the appropriate size in the bottom of the sphere to insert a covered wooden dowel. Create a bottom cube for the topiary and attach it to the other end of the covered wooden dowel. Young crafters: Have an adult help with this step.

ADHESIVE ADVICE

To give this topiary a really unique appearance, use petal points in four or more colors or patterns, and try to prevent petal points of the same color or pattern from touching each other.

CONE TOPIARY

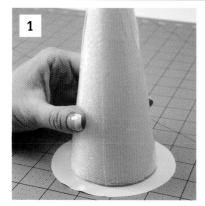

SELECT A CONE AND COVER THE BOTTOM. Select a polystyrene foam cone of the desired size and leave the plastic packaging on it (if necessary, wrap the cone in clear packaging tape). Cut a circle from a duct tape sheet that is ½" (13mm) larger than the diameter of the base of the cone. Remove the paper backing, and center the base of the cone on the sticky side of the duct tape circle.

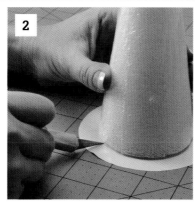

NOTCH THE TAPE. Cut notches ½" (13mm) apart in the exposed tape around the cone base with a hobby knife.

FOLD UP THE TAPE. Fold the notched pieces of tape up around the bottom edge of the cone.

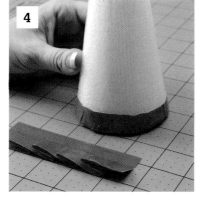

CREATE A RUFFLE. Measure the circumference of the cone where the ruffle is to be applied, and create a ruffle of the appropriate length on your work surface.

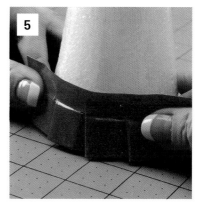

ATTACH THE RUFFLE. Peel the ruffle from your work surface and attach it along the bottom edge of the cone, wrapping it the whole way around the cone.

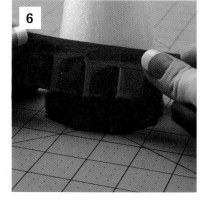

COVER THE CONE. Continue wrapping layers of ruffles around the cone until you reach the top. Then, measure the diameter of the top circle of the cone. Cut a circle of that diameter from a sheet of tape and use it to cover the top portion of the cone. Drill a hole of the appropriate size in the bottom of the cone. Create a base for the topiary, and connect the top and bottom pieces with a covered wooden dowel.

INDEX

ACQUISITION EDITOR: Peg Couch

ASSOCIATE EDITOR: Kerri Landis

EDITOR: Katie Weeber

COPY EDITORS: Paul Hambke and Heather Stauffer

COPYWRITER: Katie Weeber

COVER AND LAYOUT DESIGNER: Ashley Millhouse

PHOTOGRAPHER: Scott Kriner

PROOFREADER: Lynda Jo Runkle

INDEXER: Jay Kreider

More Great Books from Design Originals

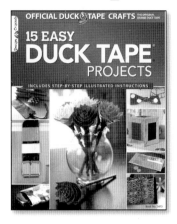

Official Duck Tape ® Craft Book
ISBN: 978-1-57421-350-8 **$8.99**
DO3473

Steampunk Fashion
ISBN: 978-1-57421-419-2 **$22.99**
DO5390

Sew Kawaii!
ISBN: 978-1-56523-568-7 **$19.95**

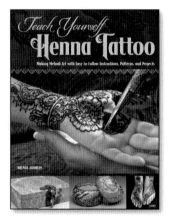

Teach Yourself Henna Tattoo
ISBN: 978-1-57421-414-7 **$19.99**
DO5385

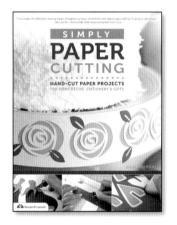

Simply Paper Cutting
ISBN: 978-1-57421-418-5 **$19.99**
DO5389

Sew Baby
ISBN: 978-1-57421-421-5 **$19.99**
DO5392

Hip Knitting
ISBN: 978-1-57421-426-0 **$12.99**
DO5397

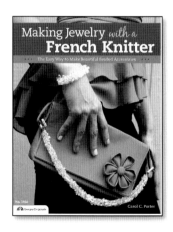

**Making Jewelry with
a French Knitter**
ISBN: 978-1-57421-363-8 **$8.99**
DO3486